THE
REFORMER'S
PLEDGE

THE REFORMER'S PLEDGE

COMPILED BY
CHÉ AHN

DESTINY IMAGE® PUBLISHERS, INC.

P.O. Box 310, Shippensburg, PA 17257-0310

"Speaking to the Purposes of God for This Generation and for the Generations to Come."

This book and all other Destiny Image, Revival Press, MercyPlace, Fresh Bread, Destiny Image Fiction, and Treasure House books are available at Christian bookstores and distributors worldwide.

For a U.S. bookstore nearest you, call 1-800-722-6774.
For more information on foreign distributors, call 717-532-3040.
Reach us on the Internet: www.destinyimage.com.

Edited by: Linda Radford

Trade Paper ISBN 13: 978-0-7684-3269-5
Hardcover ISBN: 978-0-7684-3493-4
Large Print ISBN: 978-0-7684-3494-1
Ebook ISBN: 978-0-7684-9096-1

For Worldwide Distribution, Printed in the U.S.A.

2 3 4 5 6 7 8 9 10 11 / 13 12 11

Dedication

To C. Peter Wagner, my apostle,
mentor, and spiritual father.

Acknowledgments

I am constantly amazed at the variety of ways the Lord employs to bring forth His work through us. The desire to present the Church with a call for reformation has been simmering in my spirit for several years. I wanted to challenge the Church to make a commitment to reformation that would result in action. Then two years ago, in January 2008, I attended a conference in Dallas where I heard my friend, the apostle Jim Hodges, quote from a document called "The Reformer's Creed," written by Dana Sleger. Suddenly everything came together! A creed is a statement that we bind ourselves to live by. Over the next few months, the Lord showed me ten areas that we must commit to if we want true reformation to take hold of us. The ten areas became the ten pledges that are the backbone of *The Reformer's Pledge,* which is an invitation to bind ourselves to God's reformation process.

I want to first thank Don Milam and Destiny Image Publications for believing in me and in this project. I want to thank each of the contributing authors for giving so much of their busy time and for sharing their life experience with reformation in this book. They are some of the most committed reformers I know. I also want to thank Linda Radford, my editor. She is simply amazing and has given hours of her time for this project. She is a devoted servant of Christ, and I am deeply grateful for her labor of love.

Finally, I want to give glory and honor to Jesus, who is the greatest revivalist and reformer in history!

Contents

Introduction

As a lover and disciple of Jesus Christ, I am called
to be a reformer, world changer, and history maker
(see Acts 13: 36). As a reformer, I pledge to advance
His Kingdom, fulfill the Great Commission, and
live for the glory of God. By His grace, power,
and authority, I also pledge the following...

The opening words of the Reformers Pledge go back to 1974, a year after my conversion. I was desperate to serve God, but I didn't know what my calling was. Was I called to be an evangelist like Billy Graham (who is one of my heroes in the faith), or was I called to be a pastor? So in the summer of 1974, I was really seeking God one night in prayer, asking what my calling was. It seemed like out of the blue, I heard what I call the inner audible voice of God. It was not audible to the ear, but it was so loud to my spirit man. I heard the Lord say, "I have called you to a ministry of love."

I knew this was the Lord. Besides the resounding voice, this was the last thing I was thinking about. I thought for sure He would say, "My son, I am pleased with your request. I am calling you to be the next Billy Graham!" But that is not what He said. I knew that my ultimate calling was to be a laid-down lover of Jesus and of others. Jesus said, in John 15:12-13: *"This is My commandment, that you love one another as I have loved you. Greater love has no one than this, than to lay down one's life for his friends."*

I believe every reformer must be motivated by a passionate love for God and for people in society. Even in human history, some of the great revolutions and reformations have not come about by hate and violence, but by love. Two outstanding examples come to mind. I think of Dr. Martin Luther King Jr. and his highly successful use of nonviolence in promoting the civil rights movement in the United States. I am also reminded of William Wilberforce, the great Christian abolitionist and Parliamentarian, who helped end the slave trade and ultimately slavery in Great Britain without one shot being fired.

Unfortunately, too often Christian leaders who are trying to bring reformation to society have been perceived as intolerant, right-wing conservatives without one ounce of compassion. The truth is that many of the people who are trying to bring about a positive reformation of our society are the most compassionate and loving people in society. I include the select writers of this book in the group of compassionate reformers. I am so privileged to personally know each author and consider all of them as dear friends. They are the most loving people that I know anywhere.

Most of these writers are well known in Christian circles, but for those who don't know them, let me give you my bio on each person. I would like to do it by giving you, the reader, their chapter headings and the theme of their chapter. Obviously, one could write a whole book on each chapter, so each author had to be selective to focus on what he or she is most passionate about. It is my hope that the essence of each pledge and the anointing that each writer has will be imparted to your life and bring personal reformation to you.

CHÉ AHN

Pledge 1

I will live a life of love, constantly receiving the love of my heavenly Father and, in return, loving God and loving my neighbor as myself (see Matt. 22:37-39).

Chapter 1

THE LOVE REFORMATION—JOHN ARNOTT

John Arnott is the founding pastor of Toronto Airport Christian Fellowship and is the president and founder of Catch The Fire Ministries. He is also the founder of his apostolic network called Partners in Harvest (PIH). John has one of the clearest messages on the Father's love, which is the key to truly loving both oneself and others. He encourages each of us to freely receive God's love and freely give it away. He hosted historic revival meetings for 12 years (1994 to 2006), six nights a week in his local church, which have impacted the whole world. Over 4 million people visited his church during those 12 years. John and his ministry brought revival into my life and ministry. He has been a close friend and mentor over the years. I can't think of a better person to teach on the reformation of love than John, who personifies the Father's love.

Pledge 2

I will lead a holy life, constantly growing in personal wholeness and godly character so that I will please God and not disqualify myself from fulfilling my destiny as a reformer (see 1 Pet. 1:15-16).

Chapter 2

UNASHAMEDLY HOLY—CINDY JACOBS

Cindy Jacobs, along with her husband Mike, are the founders of Generals International, an international ministry bringing reformation and healing to the nations. Cindy is a best-selling author and the host on her weekly international television show, *God Knows*. Her book *The Reformation Manifesto,* by Bethany House Publications, has been the textbook on the Reformation of society. Cindy is a prophet to the nations. She is also like a big sister to me and has been a prophet in my life. She is a board member of Harvest International Ministry (HIM), the ministry that I oversee. Cindy is also a powerful revivalist who has a strong word on holiness but brings a balanced approach to holiness without legalism.

Pledge 3

I will give myself to prayer since I am part of the house of prayer for all nations. I will intercede for those who are in authority over the seven mountains of culture. Through prayer, I will spiritually contend with all false religions and false ideologies. I will also pray for the peace of Jerusalem and pray that all of Israel will be saved (see Mark 11:17).

Chapter 3

HISTORY BELONGS TO THE INTERCESSORS—JAMES W. GOLL

James W. Goll is the president and founder of Encounter's Network. James is the best-selling author of numerous books, including *The Seer* (Destiny Image Publishers) and *The Prophetic Intercessor* (Chosen Books). James Goll is an Ephesians 4:11 seer prophet (read *The Seer*), and his entire life personifies prophetic intercession. James has consistently spoken prophetic words into my life that have been revolutionary. He is a dear friend who is on the apostolic team of HIM. He has been given a special focus to pray for those in authority and to pray for both the United States and Israel.

Pledge 4

I will contend for revival in the Church and spiritual awakening in my nation, and I will continually be filled with the power of the Holy Spirit (see Joel 2:28).

Chapter 4

GOING FROM GLORY TO GLORY—BILL JOHNSON

Bill is one of my best friends. He, too, is a best-selling author with an international ministry. He and his church, the Bethel Church in Redding, California, have been in revival for many years. What is so exciting about the revival birthed out of this local church is the transformation that is taking place in their city. One indicator of transformation is economic transformation. When I was at Fuller Seminary, I was taught that this is "redemption and lift." Wherever the Gospel of the Kingdom penetrates society, it brings redemption and lifts that society out of poverty. I have been going up to Redding each year for the past seven years, and each time I go up to Redding, I see how the city is financially prospering. Even during the recession, Bill shared with me that Redding hasn't been impacted by the recession as other cities in California have. I believe Bill is the foremost revivalist in our country. He is the perfect spokesman for this chapter on revival and reformation of society.

Pledge 5

I will contend for the rights of the unborn until abortion is illegal and rare. I will not vote for anyone who is pro-choice (see Exod. 20:13).

Chapter 5

CREATING A CULTURE OF LIFE—LOU ENGLE

What can I say about Lou? I have been in covenant relationship with him since 1983. Our families came out together to Los Angeles from the east coast. Together we saw revival come to LA, and out of that revival, we started Harvest Rock Church, Harvest International Ministry (HIM), and TheCall, an international prayer movement. Lou now serves as president of TheCall and TheCall to Conscience. God has raised up Lou to be one of the most influential prophetic voices in the pro-life movement. Lou believes that he is called to end abortion in his lifetime. In my opinion, he is a modern-day Wilberforce for the cause of the "right to life" movement.

Pledge 6

I will focus on strengthening and prioritizing my own family and will not allow the sacred covenant of marriage between a man and a woman to be constitutionally redefined (see Gen. 2:24).

Chapter 6

REFORMATION OF MARRIAGE—JIM GARLOW

Jim Garlow is the senior pastor of Skyline Wesleyan Church in San Diego and is a leading evangelical in the USA. I have known about Jim and his ministry for a number of years, but we became good friends during TheCall San Diego and during his historic leadership in the mobilization of thousands of pastors and churches in California to pass Prop 8, by a margin of 52 percent to 48 percent, in the November 2008 election. Prop 8 upheld the state definition of marriage as being between one man and one woman. In my opinion, we would have lost that ballot if Jim had not mobilized the churches to vote yes on Prop 8. Jim has been on "Larry King Live," "Dr. Phil," and "Nightline," and is heard daily on 400 radio stations with the Garlow Perspective. He is the most articulate person I know regarding this subject.

Pledge 7

I will fight racism and social injustice, care for God's planet, and do all that I can to eradicate systemic poverty through my sphere of influence (see Matt. 6:9-13).

Chapter 7

STOPPING FOR THE ONE—HEIDI BAKER

Heidi and Rolland Baker are some of my closest friends and are two of the most amazing people that I know. They are the leaders and founders of Iris Ministries and are single-handedly transforming the nation of Mozambique. They have taken seriously the mandate from Jesus to disciple a whole nation by planting over 8,000 churches in Mozambique and caring for thousands of orphans. I know no one who cares for the poor like Heidi and Rolland Baker. Not only are they feeding up to 50,000 people daily, they are also looking for ways to eradicate systemic poverty and corruption. Through the example of their lives, Rolland and Heidi have the authority to inspire others to fight injustice and systemic poverty.

Pledge 8

I will discover which of the seven mountains of culture (religion, family, business, government, education, the media, and arts and entertainment) God has designed me to climb, and I will do my part in reformation of those areas to which I am called (see Matt. 28:18-20).

Chapter 8

THE SEVEN MOUNTAIN MANDATE—LANCE WALLNAU

Lance is a dynamic and gifted speaker and is the leading authority and pioneer on the subject of reforming society. Lance is a consultant to a number of Fortune 500 companies. He is the president and founder of Lance Learning, a ministry that helps people discover their divine assignment and learn how to reach the top of the seven mountains of culture. It is safe to say that Lance's teaching on reforming society has impacted all of the authors in this book. He has been a wonderful friend and mentor to me. Trust me, there is no one better to write on this subject.

Pledge 9

I will be generous with my time, finances, gifts, and talents that God has entrusted to me to bring about public reformation of society (see Luke 19:11-26).

Chapter 9

STEWARDING FOR REFORMATION—C. PETER WAGNER

Peter is my spiritual father, mentor, and apostle. Peter Wagner and his wife, Doris, are the founders of Global Harvest Ministries. He is the founder and Chancellor Emeritus of Wagner Leadership Institute. Peter served as a professor at Fuller Seminary for over 30 years and is a prolific author. He has written over 70 books and has one of the best books on reformation of society, called *Dominion* (Chosen Books). In my opinion, Peter will go down in history as one of the great evangelical leaders of the twentieth century. He has written much on the transfer of wealth and gives an informed chapter on how wealth is necessary to reform society.

Pledge 10

I will love God's Church, walk in unity with God's people, and be in proper alignment and covering with those who are in spiritual authority in my life, beside me in serving the Lord, and entrusted to me for oversight. I will pursue unity, alignment, and righteousness within these relationships, knowing that it takes this cohesion in the Body of Christ to reform society (see Ps. 133).

Chapter 10

ALIGNING FOR REFORMATION—CHUCK PIERCE

Chuck Pierce is a person who understands apostolic alignment through practical experience; he's been aligned as a prophet with Peter Wagner's apostleship for many years. He is the founder and president of Glory of Zion International, which is a prophetic, apostolic ministry that ministers throughout the world. Now God has raised him up to lead Global Spheres, an apostolic network to bring about the reformation of society. He is a best-selling author and has a rare calling as a prophet apostle. He has impacted nations with his international ministry. He is one of the most loving and generous people that I know, and I consider it an honor to be his friend. I have the deepest love and respect for him.

It is my hope that this book will glorify God by sparking a vision for reformation, not just for the United States, but for every nation. By God's grace, some of the top reformers and thinkers have been assembled to write this book. My prayer is that you would not just receive information, but an impartation from each of these unique writers. May God raise you up to go way beyond what these authors have accomplished in bringing about revival and reformation of society.

THE REFORMER'S PLEDGE

By Ché Ahn

As a lover and disciple of Jesus Christ, I am called to be a reformer, world changer, and history maker. As a reformer, I pledge to advance His Kingdom, fulfill the Great Commission, and live for the glory of God. By His grace, power, and authority, I also pledge the following:

Pledge 1

I will live a life of love, constantly receiving the love of my heavenly Father and, in return, loving God and loving my neighbor as myself (see Matt. 22:37-39).

Pledge 2

I will lead a holy life, constantly growing in personal wholeness and godly character so that I will please God and not disqualify myself from fulfilling my destiny as a reformer (see 1 Pet. 1:15-16).

Pledge 3

I will give myself to prayer since I am part of the house of prayer for all nations. I will intercede for those who are in authority over the seven mountains of culture. Through prayer, I will spiritually contend with all false religions and false ideologies. I will also pray for the peace of Jerusalem and pray that all of Israel will be saved (see Mark 11:17).

Pledge 4

I will contend for revival in the Church and spiritual awakening in my nation, and I will continually be filled with the power of the Holy Spirit (see Joel 2:28).

Pledge 5

I will contend for the rights of the unborn until abortion is illegal and rare. I will not vote for anyone who is pro-choice (see Exod. 20:13).

Pledge 6

I will focus on strengthening and prioritizing my own family and will not allow the sacred covenant of marriage between a man and a woman to be constitutionally redefined (see Gen. 2:24).

Pledge 7

I will fight racism and social injustice, care for God's planet, and do all that I can to eradicate systemic poverty through my sphere of influence (see Matt. 6:9-13).

Pledge 8

I will discover which of the seven mountains of culture (religion, family, business, government, education, the media, and arts and entertainment) God has designed me to climb, and I will do my part to bring sustained social transformation to those areas to which I am called (see Matt. 28:18-20).

Pledge 9

I will be generous with my time, finances, gifts, and talents that God has entrusted to me to bring about public reformation of society (see Luke 19:11-26).

Pledge 10

I will love God's Church, walk in unity with God's people, and be in proper alignment and covering with those who are in spiritual authority in my life, beside me in serving the Lord, and entrusted to me for oversight. I will pursue unity, alignment, and righteousness within these relationships, knowing that it takes this cohesion in the Body of Christ to reform society (see Ps. 133).

Chapter 1

THE LOVE REFORMATION

JOHN ARNOTT

Pledge 1: I will live a life of love, constantly
receiving the love of my heavenly Father
and, in return, loving God and loving my
neighbor as myself (see Matt. 22:37-39).

I have often said that my only regret as a Christian for over 50
years now is that it took me far too long to discover the foundational
importance of the love of God. I am not talking about the theological
truth about the love of God because I certainly knew that the
Bible taught that God is love, and I probably talked about it often
enough. I am speaking about the 18-inch journey, where truth goes
from the head to the heart, where the truth is "caught" rather than
merely taught.

When you discover the deep, pervasive truth that God the Father really loves you and when you experience that love in a deep, meaningful, and powerful way, a foundational shift takes place in the inner core of your being. It allows you to love Him and others in return. Brennan Manning quotes Saint Augustine in his book, *The Furious Longing of God:* "Because You loved me, I now am lovable."[1] What a powerful summary statement! The Father's Love is indeed transforming.

THE THREE JOURNEYS

In experiencing this love connection, I often speak about three journeys: the inward journey, the upward journey, and the outward journey. The inward journey is about me and my needs—and you and your needs. It is the journey of discovering that God really cares for you, loves you, and wants the very best for your life. In other words, your needs (and mine) are important to Him, very important. It is the journey that heals the heart. The upward journey is about us loving and worshiping Him. This is also an important journey. The Father is seeking those who will worship Him in spirit and in truth (see John 4:23). It is an upward, heavenward journey of loving the Father in worship, song, and prayer. And He is seeking those who will journey upward. The outward journey is, of course, where our attention and focus is directed toward others who are the beneficiaries of our ministry toward them. This ministry may be evangelism or healing, worship or prayer, counseling or pastoral care.

I remember as a new Christian, how the emphasis was quickly refocused on the outward journey of reaching the lost and building the Church. I got the impression that my needs would be met along the way, through studying the Word and through prayer. Other than that, I should be reaching out to others. It was the outward mission that was of the uppermost importance.

So, if I had prioritized the three journeys at that time, I would have listed them in this way:

1. Outward journey—most important

2. Upward journey—needed to maintain your mission

3. Inward journey—not really needed; must die to self

It was as though the inward journey was for self-centered people who continued in carnality and did not really die to self. Therefore the inward journey was to be discouraged. It was for the "consumer Christians" and for the weak or unstable. The healthy, strong, and "really saved" didn't need a lot of personal ministry and attention and could simply get on with the outward mission. That was my perception anyway. The Great Commandment to love God with all one's strength was somewhat minimized—not theologically and biblically of course, but experientially. It didn't seem to have much relevance in the practical out workings of serving the Lord and living your life for Him. The heart issue of loving God with all one's being was certainly not seen or emphasized as the key that will bring freedom and strength to flow in the other two journeys.

So what does it look like when believers who are zealous and keen are quickly sent out on the outward mission to win the lost, but they don't have the Great Commandment down? Jesus was asked the question "What is the great commandment?" Unhesitatingly He replied, *"You shall love the Lord your God with all your heart, with all your soul, and with all your mind"* (Matt. 22:37). The second commandment is like the first; we are to love our neighbors as ourselves (see Matt. 22:39). The first commandment is love, and the second commandment is love. It is important that we see here how Jesus focused on heart issues. He focused on loving God, loving others, and loving ourselves, with care, compassion, and sincerity. The great commandment is to love. We must have a sincere, genuine, heartfelt love for God, for neighbor, and for self. It has been said that if we do not love ourselves, we will not have the capacity to love others, and that includes loving God.

So the inward journey is very important after all. God wants to take us on it—just for us, just for our benefit. And it is because He loves us just for who we are and not for the work we can do. The peace and power of the Holy Spirit has come to help people in their distress, to bind up the brokenhearted, to heal the bruised, and to set the captives free (see Isa. 61:1). God wants to love us to life deep in the core of our being so that we can say like St. Augustine: "Because He loved me, I now am lovable." Knowing we are loved sets us free to be true worshipers, worshiping in spirit and in truth and motivated by His love rather than fear (see 1 John 4:18). With this healing and freedom under our belts, so to speak, we now become more motivated than ever to bring the life, power, and love of the Kingdom of God to a broken, needy, and dying generation. Love is by far a stronger motivator than fear and religious duty. Love will take you the extra mile again and again.

THE JOURNEY BEGINS

I experienced my first real brush with the love of God in the ministry of Kathryn Kuhlman. The delivery of her messages was usually very quiet, sometimes even in a whisper. Yet the messages were rich in content and amazingly transparent. Then suddenly, in the midst of her message, almost without warning, she would transition into a string of precise words of knowledge, calling out miracles for MS, spinal conditions, heart disease, or cancer. Streams of people would begin to flow forward to testify of the healing and supernatural work that God had just done in their bodies. Very often when they gave their testimonies at the microphone, you heard them say that they were, of course, very thankful for the physical healing. However, the great work that the Father had also done in their hearts often almost overshadowed the physical healing! As the Holy Spirit had come upon them, they had received a revelation of the Father's love that went deep within and was life-changing. Through that ministry, I began to see what it looks like when people are loved just for who they are and not because of what they had achieved. And Kathryn really did genuinely love them with the love of God that flowed richly out of her.

It was then, as I began to see God's love demonstrated in the life and ministry of Jesus, that I began to desire this love in my own life. Jesus was not merely a man on a mission to seek and save the lost, but He genuinely cared for people. He healed the sick, even when it cost Him dearly for healing on the Sabbath day (see Matt. 12:9-14). His mission was important, of course, but He really cared about people, their hurts, their needs, and their potential to love once their hearts were healed and unlocked.

For me, Kathryn Kuhlman was a breath of fresh air. She was so different from other healing evangelists who often brought strong exhortations for the sick and needy to "believe." She reminded her listeners of the unconditional love of God that would fall upon them by the power of the Holy Spirit and bring healing, freedom, and new life.

ISRAEL: THE JOURNEY CONTINUES

My next encounter with God's love was on my very first trip to Israel in 1974. I went fasting and praying, only to be completely disarmed by the ministry of David DuPlessis. I had never encountered someone so embracing of all denominations of Christians. "Even if they have different doctrine than you," he would plead, "can't you love them? They are walking in the only light that they know!" His words would cut me to the heart. They exposed my self-righteousness. I realized that I had been on a diligent quest for truth, but truth for truth's sake. Suddenly I began to realize that the real truth is that God is love. He wants us rooted and grounded in love so that we can comprehend how big His Kingdom really is (see Eph. 3:17-18).

The Kingdom of God is actually a Kingdom of love. The trinity of God is a relationship of love. Father God is love; the Son is His beloved; and the Spirit is the bond of love between them. That truth began to sink deep into my heart and spirit on that trip to Israel. I became undone with waves of the Father's love relentlessly washing over me again and again and again. Not only could I scarcely sleep for the entire week there, but at times I wondered if I would live through the successive waves of intense love and power that were crashing down upon my soul! His love had found me.

Later, following a mission to Indonesia in 1980, my wife, Carol, and I received a call into ministry, and we planted our first church in her hometown of Stratford, Ontario, Canada. We wanted a *love church*—one that would not only win the lost, but one that would also love and care for people. We wanted to see people find freedom from besetting habits and sins and walk in the freedom and love that God had intended for them. It was easier said than done, but I kept reminding the many youth that we had won off the streets, "God loves you just the way you are. But He loves you too much to leave you the way you are so He will take you step by step and from glory to glory." We discovered that prayer, Bible studies, and the Christian disciplines alone were not usually enough to change today's hurting, wounded people into loving disciples of Christ. We needed something more!

AN INTRODUCTION TO THE
FATHER HEART OF GOD

Through friends at YWAM (Youth With A Mission), I learned of the ministry of Jack Winter. When I asked what he taught on, they told me, "He talks about the Father heart of God." That phrase sounded strange to me, but because I trusted these good friends, we acted on their recommendation and asked Jack Winter to come and hold meetings at our little church in Stratford. I will never forget Jack's gentle, loving demeanor. And then he read John 14, verse 6 to us. *"Jesus said to him, 'I am the way, the truth, and the life. No one comes to the Father except through Me.'"*

"Where is it that we are going?" he asked. I wanted to say "To Heaven," but that is not really what the text says. Jack clearly pointed out that we were going to the Father. He was our destination. And for some reason, I didn't particularly want to go there. I had read that verse of Scripture multitudes of times. I loved that passage. Yet I always used it to point out that Jesus was the only way to Heaven. Apart from Jesus (who is God in human form), there is no other savior. I was very comfortable with Jesus; I loved Jesus. I loved Him for His miracles and power. I loved Him because of His amazing words of teaching and wisdom, and I loved Him because He was not just a great leader on a mission, but one who genuinely loved and cared about people. But I did not really know the Father.

I assumed that the Father was inflexible and demanding. I read the Old Testament and saw there that one false move would cost you your life. To me, therefore, the Father was a good one to keep your distance from! He was like the big cop or the big Pharisee in the sky. I never thought of being close to him as an intimate Daddy (which is what *Abba* means). Slowly and carefully, Jack Winter unpacked this powerful, intimate truth to us (it was revolutionary teaching in the early 1980s).

The passage in Luke 15 about the prodigal son was another text about the Father Heart of God that Jack brought to life for us. It was the Father who was longing for that wayward son to return. It was the Father who welcomed him home. It was the Father who threw the party and celebrated. Fortunately, that young man was not first met by the older brother. In those days, that older brother would have been a picture of me—full of self righteousness and reasons why, since the prodigal had received and wasted his inheritance, there was no more place for him at home. This is perhaps the best illustration of the Father's love in all of Scripture, and it is arguably the most powerful of all the parables that Jesus told.

Of course, there are many other Scriptures that clearly teach that God is love. Allow me to list a few of them.

> *And the Lord passed before him and proclaimed, "**The Lord, the Lord** God, merciful and gracious, longsuffering, and abounding in goodness and truth"* (Exodus 34:6).

> *In this the **love of God** was manifested toward us, that God has sent His only begotten Son into the world, that we might live through Him* (1 John 4:9).

Matthew 22:37 states very clearly that we are to love the Lord with all our heart and soul. John 3:16 is perhaps the clearest and most well-known verse in Scripture: *"For God so loved the world, that He gave His only begotten Son, that whoever believes in Him should not perish but have everlasting life."* It all happened because God the Father so loved. That is as clear as anything. I wonder why it took me so long to really "get it."

CONNECTING WITH THE FATHER'S LOVE

I have concluded that our hearts are slow learners. Without intentional and pointed teaching, we are likely to miss this foundational truth for a very long time. I have already discussed Matthew 22:37— the commandment to love the Lord with all our hearts and souls. Jesus called it the Great Commandment. But what does it look like when that is actually taking place? I think it looks more like Mary at the feet of Jesus, than Martha working in the kitchen. The truth of God's love often gets reinterpreted to mean "serve and work for Him, thereby showing and demonstrating your love to God." But actually loving God means loving Him with a heart and soul connection. Your emotions are engaged and fully in play. Working for God is good too, but it is an entirely different issue.

Why not take a moment right now and begin to connect with the love of God. Quiet yourself down. Allow your heart to think and meditate on His faithfulness to you over the last few weeks and months; then let your heart rise to honor and thank Him for His faithful love.

When you and I experience the Father's love in our hearts and are convinced of its biblical truth and certainty, we can begin to rest and be comfortable in Father's presence. He becomes a safe place for us, and we can begin to tell Him the secrets of our hearts. We can begin to take the walls of protection and self-preservation down and allow Him to bind up our broken hearts, heal the bruises, and set us free from our captivity (see Isa. 61:1). I honestly believe that it is from this safe place in the Father's arms and heart, that we can actually open up to receive healing from life's hurts. It is in our identity as sons and daughters, knowing and having experienced the Father's love as a present reality, that we feel safe enough to get real about the issues in our hearts. As we open up to His trinitarian presence, healing comes deeply in.

In John 1:18, Scripture teaches that Jesus came to reveal the Father and show us what He is truly like. We see that He is just like Jesus. In John 14:9, Jesus tells Phillip, *"...He who has seen Me, has seen the Father...."* Likewise, Hebrews 1:3 tells us that the Son is the exact representation of the Father's being. So then, the Father is exactly like Jesus, and vice versa. All of the kind works toward broken lives were really the Father doing those works through Jesus the Son.

> *Don't you believe that I am in the Father, and that the Father is in Me? The words I say to you are not just My own. Rather, it is the Father, living in Me, who is doing His work* (John 14:10 NIV).

So it is really the Father (through Jesus) who touches and heals the leper (see Matt. 8:1-4). It is really the Father who cares for and delivers the demonized fortune teller (see Acts 16:16-18). It is really the Father who multiplies the food and feeds the hungry multitude (see Luke 9:10-17). For the very same reasons that I loved and appreciated Jesus, I now began to love and appreciate the Father as well—just for who He is.

When we understand His love for us, the Father becomes our safe place. We can run to Him, dwell in the secret place of His heart, and hide safely under the shadow of His powerful presence (see Ps. 91). He becomes our shepherd, and goodness and mercy shall follow us all the days of our lives (see Ps. 23). We begin to cry "Abba, Daddy" as we journey from being orphans to sons and daughters (see Rom. 8:15-17).

Ask God to deepen this revelation in your life. It is the very foundation that Ephesians 3:17-19 is talking about. We need to be rooted and grounded in love so that we may be able to comprehend how *big* this revelation is and then be filled with all the fullness of God. It is reiterated in First John 3:1:

How great is the love the Father has lavished on us,
that we should be called children of God! And that is
what we are! The reason the world does not know us is
that it did not know Him (1 John 3:1 NIV).

The invitation is to get to know Him! Being close to the Father enables us to begin to hear His voice. His voice speaks tenderly and truthfully to us, calling us into His heart. He calls us into deeper healing and into increasing fruitfulness.

Recently in Accra, a city in Ghana, West Africa, I met a young man who was revolutionized by the Father's love. His name is Eben (short for Ebenezer). His father died when he was 6 years old. He was immediately sent to live with his grandparents and did not see his mother again for 20 years. He lost his father and his mother in one day and has been looking for a father ever since. Later he gave his life to Jesus and began attending a wonderful church called Calvary Temple, led by pastor Anthony Cudjoe. The pastor, noticing Eben's sincerity and commitment, began to draw him closer personally and fathered him in many ways.

While we were there, we prayed for Eben many times; each time he would go out under the power of the Spirit, going deeper and deeper. About the third time, he was so deeply touched that he was undone and could not speak. Finally, he was able to share with me what had happened. While he was in the Spirit, the Father came to him, took him in His arms, and held him. Then He told him, "I am your Father; look to Me. I am the one you have been looking for all of your life." Needless to say, that young man's countenance was transformed as he went from being an orphan to being a son. That is the inward journey, the 18-inch journey during which truth goes from the head to the heart. And when you finally make that journey, you know, that you know, that you know!

LIVING BY HIS LOVE

I believe that this guiding principle of love was the very thing that Jesus lived by. He loved His Father and would leave powerful, successful healing and revival meetings to go off into the mountains and be alone with Him. In Luke 4:42, He left the crowds and went into a solitary place—the place of prayer. There He had the sweet communion of His Father's presence, and I believe He loved it. It was nurture, relationship, and strength to His soul. He was loving God, His Father, with all His heart and with all His soul. On the strength of that, he had the inner strength and anointing to go and minister to the needy. But not just that, He had an overflowing love that enabled Him not only to minister, but to truly love and care for all the people. They were not merely a project for Jesus to reach. He loved them. It was actually the Father's love overflowing through Him.

Let's consider the story of the woman anointing His feet from Luke 7:36-50:

> Now one of the Pharisees invited Jesus to have dinner with him, so He went to the Pharisee's house and reclined at the table. When a woman who had lived a sinful life in that town learned that Jesus was eating at the Pharisee's house, she brought an alabaster jar of perfume, and as she stood behind Him at His feet weeping, she began to wet His feet with her tears. Then she wiped them with her hair, kissed them and poured perfume on them.
>
> When the Pharisee who had invited Him saw this, he said to himself, "If this man were a prophet, He would

know who is touching Him and what kind of woman she is—that she is a sinner."

Jesus answered him, "Simon, I have something to tell you." "Tell me, teacher," he said.

"Two men owed money to a certain moneylender. One owed him five hundred denarii, and the other fifty. Neither of them had the money to pay him back, so he canceled the debts of both. Now which of them will love him more?"

Simon replied, "I suppose the one who had the bigger debt canceled." "You have judged correctly," Jesus said.

Then He turned toward the woman and said to Simon, "Do you see this woman? I came into your house. You did not give Me any water for My feet, but she wet My feet with her tears and wiped them with her hair. You did not give Me a kiss, but this woman, from the time I entered, has not stopped kissing My feet. You did not put oil on My head, but she has poured perfume on My feet. Therefore, I tell you, her many sins have been forgiven—for she loved much. But he who has been forgiven little loves little."

Then Jesus said to her, "Your sins are forgiven." The other guests began to say among themselves, "Who is this who even forgives sins?" Jesus said to the woman, "Your faith has saved you; go in peace" (Luke 7:36-50 NIV).

This is a fascinating story. Jesus was invited to the house of a Pharisee named Simon. I suspect that it was a private dinner arranged for Jesus and His disciples. Suddenly an uninvited guest arrives, goes directly to the feet of Jesus, and begins crying, wetting His feet with her tears, and drying them with her hair. He neither says nor does anything to stop her. She continues, anointing His feet with perfumed oil and repeatedly kissing His feet.

As you can imagine, people were really wondering what was going on. Why was this great Prophet allowing this woman to continue? Jesus, discerning Simon's thoughts and questions, spoke up finally and told Simon a parable of two debtors, one who owes a little and the other who owes much. When the lender in His story forgave and canceled both debts, Jesus asked, *"Which of them will love him more?"* *"I suppose the one who had the bigger debt canceled,"* was the right answer.

Then Jesus made His point. *"Do you see this woman?"* She had outdone Simon with honoring and love. She had poured out extravagant love, but the point was that Jesus had allowed her to do it. In the face of all the disapproval of the other guests, he allowed a sinful woman to carry on kissing His feet because accepting the honor and love from this poor woman was more important to Him than receiving the approval of His host. Jesus would happily risk His own reputation for the sake of allowing one poor soul to find love, acceptance, and forgiveness.

I can only imagine how uncomfortable I would have been in that set of circumstances—a sinful woman crying and kissing my feet in front of all the others. I can just feel their respect evaporating and their questions rising. That sort of thing is just not done. But Jesus has a different and higher set of values. Giving and receiving love is by far the most important thing. So He allowed this woman to weep her way through to peace and salvation while He stared down the questions and looks of disapproval. What a champion for the Kingdom of love!

It is stories like this one and the one about the prodigal son that shout the message of God the Father's love so very loud and clear to us all. The wayward, wasteful son was not met with what he deserved, but encountered a radical all-forgiving love from his father. The wayward woman met the most incredible, healing love that she had ever encountered. This is the challenge for me, and for you; will we begin to comprehend and then walk in this kind of love?

It is the kind of love that Paul speaks about in First Corinthians chapter 13.

> *Love is patient, love is kind. It does not envy, it does not boast, it is not proud. It is not rude, it is not self-seeking, it is not easily angered, it keeps no record of wrongs. Love does not delight in evil but rejoices with the truth. It always protects, always trusts, always hopes, always perseveres. Love never fails* (1 Corinthians 13:4-8a NIV).

I cannot help but reiterate the words of the beloved apostle in First John 3:1, *"How great is the love the Father has lavished on us, that we should be called children of God! And that is what we are!…"* The entire Book of First John talks about the Father's love over and over again. I encourage you to read it, meditate on it, and soak in it until you get it. Once you get it, then walk in God's love and give it away.

Someone once said that the main thing is "keeping the main thing the main thing." And this is the main thing for every child of God: loving the Lord with all your heart and soul. That is the motivation that changes hearts and circumstances. The love of God, continuing to go deep into our inner beings, will transform our own ability to love Him in return and to love others even as we love ourselves. The upward journey of worship and prayer and the outward journey of mission and fruitfulness are far better served with a heart set on fire with the flame of love—the love of a loving Father who is ruler over the Kingdom of love.

Chapter 2

UNASHAMEDLY HOLY

CINDY JACOBS

Pledge 2: I will lead a holy life, constantly growing in personal wholeness and godly character so that I will please God and not disqualify myself from fulfilling my destiny as a reformer (see 1 Pet. 1:15-16).

AN ENCOUNTER WITH HOLINESS

Many years ago, while in a time of prayer, I had a visitation from the Lord. At that time, I had been seeking to know Him on a deeper and more intimate level. I wasn't alone in the room, but as it happens, when the Lord makes His presence felt, you could be in a crowd of thousands and still, somehow, be completely caught up in a one-on-one experience.

During the visitation, I saw the Lord's eyes looking into my own. I wish I could describe those eyes in human terms, but I simply cannot. I could not tell you their color or size. Instead, what I can try to do is describe their impact on me as a person.

I'm sure that this kind of encounter with God is a fearsome thing. I often think of that when people speak His name without considering whom they are talking about or when they use His name as a curse. All I can say is that after that time I will never again be able to use His name in a light and joking manner. Of course, there will be a day when all will experience the full force of Him, and at that moment, every knee in the universe will bow and declare Him King of kings (see Rom. 14:9-12).

I said that I gazed into His eyes, but it would be more appropriate to say that He looked into mine. His eyes pierced my soul and my life like radar, and I became deeply and profoundly aware of my state of imperfection—that my highest thoughts could not match His and my deepest moment of love for another person could not come close to His love for me.

The difference between our states—His perfect and Holy and mine as a sinful person—became evident. I remember groaning under that gaze and heard my voice cry out at last, "Please, God, no more!" I thought if He continued looking into my eyes that I would expire. In short, I could not bear the weight of His glory or the knowledge of my own imperfections that I was experiencing in my present human state before His holy presence.

My favorite biblical prophet, Isaiah, had a similar encounter with God, and he described it like this:

> "Doom! It's Doomsday! I'm as good as dead! Every word
> I've ever spoken is tainted—blasphemous even! And

the people I live with talk the same way, using words
that corrupt and desecrate. And here I've looked God
in the face! The King! God-of-the-Angel-Armies!"

Then one of the angel-seraphs flew to me. He held a
live coal that he had taken with tongs from the altar.
He touched my mouth with the coal and said, "Look.
This coal has touched your lips. Gone your guilt Your
sins wiped out" (Isaiah 6:5-7 TM).

During those moments when I gazed into His eyes, however, the overarching emotion I experienced was that, in spite of my present state, *God loves me.* He loves me completely, without reservation, and with purity and holiness, and He longs for my communion with Him. There was no condemnation, and I now know that someday I will see Him face-to-face and not desire to look away.

Those kinds of visitations mark one's soul. The deep imprint it made upon mine is this: *I want to be holy as He is Holy for He is the lover of my soul.*

HOLINESS AND REFORMATION

Why do we include the subject of holiness in a book on reformation? Holiness is important. We are commanded to pursue it because without it we won't see the Lord (see Heb. 12:14). This is one reason why this chapter is critical. There can be no true reformation without holiness at its base, whether it is the reformation of a soul or the reformation of a nation. We need to know how to pursue His holiness.

Around ten years ago, I began to prophesy that a new holiness movement was going to break out that would sweep the face of the earth. I am personally committed with all of my heart to seeing this happen.

It seems that the boundaries of acceptable behavior in our culture, and more sadly, the Church, have moved concerning what is holy and what is not. Actions that used to be avoided or were shameful are now primetime fare on television reality shows. I believe we need to have a holiness movement to give a radical course adjustment to the slippery slope that we are going down today in many nations. We need young firebrands to rise up with a cry in their hearts of holiness.

My friend Sergio Scataglini, the Argentinean revival leader who has turned cities upside down with his preaching, says we must have 100 percent holiness—no less! During a dramatic visitation from God concerning holiness, the Lord told him, "Nobody gets up in the morning, prepares a cup of coffee, and then puts a drop of poison in it, stirs and drinks it." But the Lord showed him that many people in the Church do exactly this. They allow drops of poison like bitterness, unforgiveness, and entertainment-generated lustful thoughts into their hearts and minds. Without a doubt, this small quota of daily sin is destroying them. No one would consider buying a bottle of mineral water with a label that reads: "98% Pure Mineral Water, 2% Sewage Water." Yet many Christians have allowed spiritual sewage water to seep into their lives.[1]

Often in today's society, the Church represents only a subset of current culture, and we are only slightly better than the world. We may not be having an extramarital affair, but our minds flirt with lust as we watch movies that are filled with deeply suggestive innuendos. For the sake of an "entertainment experience," we are drinking poison, and it builds up in our souls. We need to move our boundaries of acceptable behavior back to God's original standards of conduct for us!

In order to comprehend the magnitude of course correction needed in our culture, we must see a generation of Holy Revolutionaries who are radically different and who are standard bearers for purity. These Holy Revolutionaries that I foresee are unashamedly holy. Holiness is their passion, and they are pursuing it with their whole heart, soul, and mind. Let's start a counterculture movement that will absolutely shift our culture back to righteousness and justice! (I have to watch it or I will preach this chapter rather than simply write it. This subject gets me so fired up!)

HOLINESS AS A RESPONSE TO GOD'S LOVE

Many times when the subject of holiness comes up, I see a reaction from people who grew up under intense legalism. To them, holiness represents a religious system and is just another word for bondage. They think of a list of don'ts and personal repression rather than a love relationship with the King.

When I think of the desire for purity as a response to God's love, I think of my marriage to my husband, Mike. As of this writing, we have been married 36 years. This morning he was dancing around the bathroom singing me a love song and pestering me for one hug, and then he wanted a kiss, and then he wanted another. You have to love a guy like that!

The sweet part of this is that I never worry that Mike will have an affair and cheat on me with another woman—ever. He feels the same way about me with another man. How can we both be so assured? Because I love him and he loves me, and our love draws a line of faithfulness to each other that we will not cross.

This is the picture of how I love Jesus, my bridegroom. He is up there singing over me in Heaven, making preparations for a big wedding. Would I cheat Him by unholy acts? That makes no sense. This is how I see the new holiness movement—it is a love song of worship and a day-to-day walk of loving God, my future husband. When I see Him, I want to know that I kept myself pure and unblemished by holy living. I want to have a clean conscience, knowing that I did not sin against Him.

This message burns in my heart! It is like spiritual marriage counseling. Of course, because our heavenly bridegroom is God, we must never forget that it is a very serious, eternal problem if we sin against Him. The Bible is the preparation manual for our relationship with God, and it is full of holiness instruction.

THE CALL TO HOLINESS

According to Jerry Bridges, author of *The Pursuit of Holiness*, the word *holy* in various forms occurs more than 600 times in the Bible. One entire Book, Leviticus, is devoted to the subject, and the idea of holiness is woven elsewhere throughout the fabric of Scripture.[2] A.W. Pink said, "Holiness....consists of that internal change or renovation of our souls whereby our minds, affections and wills are brought into harmony with God."[3]

Perhaps one of our major problems is that we have a very casual attitude toward what God considers sin. Somehow in our culture sin has been trivialized to the status of a "little white lie." It is so unpopular to preach on the subject of holiness that many people who attend church today have no idea they need to be abstinent and live a pure life. In short, they don't know what is sinful and what is not because oftentimes we as Christian leaders have not taught them.

God is looking for a generation of reformers who are unashamed to be holy! I don't know how many of our youth tell me that they are mocked publicly if someone finds out that they are virgins. Being a virgin before marriage should be a badge of honor. God is looking for a sweeping move of holiness that will shift campus culture to such an extent that it becomes the norm to keep oneself pure before marriage and to get married rather than live together.

The Bible says that we are to be holy as He is holy (see 1 Pet. 1:16). This is a commandment, not a mere suggestion. I like how The Message Bible states this in verses 13-16:

*So roll up your sleeves, put your mind in gear, be totally ready to receive the gift that's coming when Jesus arrives. Don't lazily slip back into those old grooves of evil, doing just what you feel like doing. You didn't know any better then, you do now. As obedient children, let yourselves be pulled into a way of life shaped by God's life, a life energetic and blazing with holiness. God said, "**I am holy, now you be holy**"* (1 Peter 1:13-16 TM).

It is time to ask yourself the question, "Am I ashamed of being holy? Does my life blaze a path of holiness for others to see and emulate?" One day I was pondering this subject of holiness when I had an amazing revelation about God.

He is the **Holy** Spirit.

He could have called Himself the magnificent spirit, the kind spirit, the tender spirit, the amazing spirit, or the glorious spirit, yet He chose the title Holy Spirit.

He chose to call Himself that because it is absolutely the most important attribute that He wants to manifest through us. The more we become like Him and become spirit-controlled, the holier we will become. I absolutely want to be like Him.

Since God has revealed how important it is to be holy through so many portions of Scripture, we should give a great deal of prayer and study to the subject. Consider, for instance, the 24 elders in Heaven who bow down eternally before the throne. They are crying out, "Holy, holy, holy," not "glory, glory, glory." I learned this truth from the writings of Bible teacher and well-known author, Joy Dawson.

The truth is that most people in our societies today really want Christians to act like Christians. There is a longing they have to see us live what we say we believe. When we start living a holy life before

God and people through counter-cultural purity and holiness, it will change both us and our nations.

We need a reformation back to a biblical worldview concerning a passion for holiness so we can become godly reformers and role models. C. Peter Wagner has written an excellent book titled *Radical Holiness for Radical Living.* He says, "I would not doubt for a moment that God is holy, but I also believe that you and I can be holy as well. This is not an unattainable dream; it can be a present-day reality in your life and mine."[4]

BECOMING HOLY

How does one get started on the path to become holy? Developing a deep sense of the reverential fear of God is a good place to begin. *The fear of the Lord is to hate evil* (Pro. 8:13a).

Joy Dawson, whom I mentioned earlier, makes some excellent distinctions between moral living and true holiness in her book *Intimate Friendship with God: Through Understanding the Fear of the Lord.* In it, Joy Dawson says this about being holy:

> The more we study the holiness of God from His Word, the more we will understand the extent of His hatred of sin. God has no tolerance toward sin; therefore, He will not compromise with it. Sin is abhorrent to His very nature.
>
> No matter how unholy we are now, or how impossible it may seem for us to become holy, if we have committed our lives to the Lord Jesus Christ and He is living within us, we need to remember that He is holy. If we chose to walk in obedience to revealed truth and the

next thing He tells us to do, His holy life will start to manifest through us.[5]

Her book on intimate friendship with God is very high on the list of books that have had the most impact on me. In the book, she describes four different levels of our attitudes toward sin. At the first, most basic, and selfish level, it is the fear of negative consequence, not any reverential fear of God that is the primary motivator:

> **Level One:** The person does not sin because the consequences are too great. This person lusts after someone else in his or her heart but does not commit the sin of adultery or fornication with his or her body because of the consequences being too great. Or he may hate someone else and wish that person were dead, but does not murder him because of the consequences. Obviously, there is no hatred of evil and, therefore, no fear of the Lord.

> At the second level, the person is concerned about appearances, but there is no deep conviction about the sinfulness of sin. The emphasis is on "looking good" to self and others, but the person remains largely unchanged within.

> **Level Two:** The person who lives by the Golden Rule, because he wants peace at any price and cannot understand anyone who is so radical that he would try to change the status of his life or anyone else's. This person can be full of the sins of selfishness and self-righteousness without being aware of it. He may go to church regularly every Sunday and give his tithes,

pay his bills, grow six cabbages and give one over the fence to his neighbor. He often does good deeds. If you came up to him and said, "Do you fear the Lord?" he would be most indignant that you would even ask such a question of him.

If you asked him: "How long has it been since you spent more than an hour in prevailing prayer for the lost souls? What concerns have you for the unreached millions in the world?" In all honesty he would have to answer, "Very little or none at all." There is no fear of the Lord manifest in these sins of selfishness, prayerlessness, self-centeredness, complacency, and self-righteousness. There is no acknowledgment, let alone any hatred, of these sins in the person who lives on this level.

The third level contains many well-meaning Christians who want to cease from sin, but find themselves falling into the same sins repeatedly. They have a deeper awareness of sin and its more subtle manifestations, but are not yet fully identified with Christ in hating sin. Joy continues:

Level Three: The sincere Christian who earnestly desires to please the Lord Jesus Christ. He does not want to sin and is deeply concerned when besetting sins are in his life. He wishes he could find an answer as to why he is always confessing over and over again the same sins. Perhaps he commits the sins of criticism and of judging others; the sins of pride, always drawing attention to himself in conversation; the sins of unbelief in being unable to trust God, as manifest in fear, doubt and disobedience. Or maybe it is the sins of lust, covetousness, jealousy, or resentment—to God or man. He is deeply concerned and longs for freedom.

At the fourth level the person walks in the fear of the Lord. He or she is intimately acquainted with God and hates sin, even as God hates it.

> **Level Four:** The person who has the fear of the Lord upon him hates sin; therefore, he seldom sins. If he does, there is a quick awareness of sin, immediate repentance and a willingness to humble himself before others if directed by the Holy Spirit to do so.[6]

There are two other special verses that I think tie this all together and give us a deeper biblical understanding of the role of the fear of the Lord in living a holy life:

1. *Fear-of-God deflects evil* (Proverbs 16:6b TM).

2. *The friendship of the Lord is for those who fear Him* (Psalm 24:14 NRSV).

As we continuously walk in the reverential fear of the Lord, our aversion to sin grows and actually deflects evil temptation. We find ourselves in deepening intimacy with God as we develop a true friendship with Him. Sin has no more allure for us. He has become our all-consuming desire!

I love being a friend of God. However, my friendship doesn't manifest in my taking His friendship for granted. I love Him, but I also fear Him and worship Him. I believe that one of the reasons we aren't salt and light in our nations today is that even in the Church there is no fear of the Lord.

HOLY JUDGMENT BEGINS AT THE HOUSE OF GOD

In order to bring about a massive reformation, we must first see a respect for God's awesome role, not only as a friend, but also as the creator and authority over all. He makes the rules. He is God, and we are not, and He must be obeyed. It is Holy to obey God totally, all the time, not just when we feel like it or personally think it is right.

This respect and obedience, of course, has to begin in the Church.

It's judgment time for God's own family. We're first in line... (1 Peter 4:17 TM). Other translations say that judgment must begin at the house of God. We have no moral authority to change our nations until we first become holy in the Church. I realize that many people who claim to be Christians hide behind the fact or use the excuse of hypocrisy in the Church as an explanation of why they do not serve God. We need to focus on personal holiness and stop giving them any more excuses!

I believe that one of the first requirements of a reformer is to reach level four of Joy Dawson's list! We need to live a life where we rarely sin, and if we do, we are sensitive to the conviction of the Holy Spirit, and we quickly repent. This is also Peter Wagner's premise in his book on radical holiness.

Holiness is one of the most important aspects of being a born-again reformer of nations. In my book *The Reformation Manifesto,* I write on the subject of the Great Commission mandate to disciple and teach nations (see Matt. 28:19-20). The bedrock foundation of being a biblical discipler is to understand that we have a holy mandate to reform our nations into conformity with the original design of God. The earth belongs to God; therefore, our nations' laws, governments, entertainment, educational systems, and so forth should please God. Holy reformers will work to infuse the biblical worldview into every aspect of society. It is a moral mandate.[7]

We will never be able to radically reform and transform our nations without personal holiness. Once we are living a holy life, our passions should extend our efforts to bring a culture of holiness in the daily life of our nations. I am not talking about a theocracy, but a nation where all are free to come to Christ of their own free will. However, we should be active on every level of society to see that the laws, school systems, medical practices, and so forth conform to God's plan for the world.

Holiness needs to extend beyond our own personal behavior to influence what our nations manifest as societies. We need a move of corporate holiness that includes a sweeping move of ethical reformation that will eradicate systemic corruption. My South African friend, Graham Power, the founder of The Global Day of Prayer, has started a movement to get people to sign a pledge to commit to being unashamedly ethical. Here are the points on their commitment forms:

INDIVIDUAL COMMITMENT FORM

1. To be entirely truthful in all I say.

2. To be faithful to my family relationships.

3. To do nothing out of selfish ambition or deceit,
   but to look out for the interests of others.

4. To refuse to elicit, accept, or pay any bribes, and to report those who do.

5. To be a diligent leader without being harsh, and to pay my staff what is just and fair.

6. To be a peacemaker.

7. To do my work wholeheartedly.

8. To submit myself to just and ethical governing authorities.

9. To remember the poor by investing generously and sacrificially in the broader community,

10. To collaborate with my peers to impact our community and nation.[8]

THE COMING HOLINESS REFORMATION

A sweeping move of God is coming that is like a tsunami flood that will usher many into the Body of Christ. These people will become an army that begins the reformation back to God, at least in the United States. This will fulfill the vision of John Winthrop, first governor of the Massachusetts Bay Colony, that the new nation would become a city set on a hill, an example to all the nations.[9] Some nations have never had a biblical foundation, and God will raise up leaders with a passion to establish one in their generation.

Only when we believers live as a holy nation will we become the leaven our country needs for a reformation (see Exod. 19:5-6). Satan has tried to take away our moorings through liberal theology and teaching based on Darwin's theory of evolution that imply that the Bible is only a book about God, not the inerrant word of God. We need to restore the belief that God spoke His revealed will through inspiration in Scripture, and He means to be obeyed. We need to embrace the Bible as the inerrant Word of God.

Every successive generation needs to conduct a spiritual assessment of the condition of their times and answer the call to correct any slide away from biblical truth. Reformers like British abolitionist William Wilberforce in the nineteenth century not only fought against the sin of slavery but also called for a "reformation of manners." This reformation was a return to biblical truth and called the citizens of Britain to live according to God's standards. We urgently need those with a Wilberforce call today. Who knows, maybe you, the reader, are one who will answer the call?

Holiness is on the hearts of many today. There is a new mandate to preach against sin and to see sinners converted with holy fire—like the Cane Ridge Revivals in the early 1800s, where sinners fell under the power of God and got up gloriously saved. We are entering a day where the fear of the Lord is going to fall in meetings. Sinners will have visions of the holiness of God and become gripped by the fact that they are sinners and need the sanctifying power of the Gospel to change them. We urgently need another Great Awakening to sweep the nations of the earth, calling sinners to repentance.

I am thankful to those denominations that have traditionally had a focus on holiness. They have made significant contributions to our understanding of holiness and its centrality in our relationship with God. Even these groups are meeting to revive their messages on holy living. We all need to refocus and intently pursue holiness with God.

This is what I foresee: God is going to anoint preachers with a holiness message that will sweep the nations with His holy fire. There will be deep conviction of sin as young revivalists are raised up with a passion both to walk in holiness and preach holiness. They will go forth with a moral imperative that righteousness exalts a nation (see Prov. 14:34).

These revivalists are not just going to be preaching in the usual places that we have known historically. They will preach through the films they make, the songs they sing, the art they paint. From the pulpit to the senate floor, from shopping malls to the universities of the land, from their backyards to the street corners, they will usher in a new sweeping holiness movement that will rush across the face of the earth.

These revivalists will preach through feeding the poor and fight human trafficking of every type. They will believe in holy causes such as eradicating systemic poverty. They will be miracle workers and abortion fighters. This new breed of revivalists will love God with all of their hearts, souls, and minds (see Matt. 22:37). They will not be stopped, even if they are mocked, arrested, put in jail, or martyred.

They will be unashamedly holy!

Chapter 3

HISTORY BELONGS TO
THE INTERCESSORS

JAMES W. GOLL

Pledge 3: I will give myself to prayer since I
am part of the house of prayer for all nations.
I will intercede for those who are in authority
over the seven mountains of culture. Through
prayer, I will spiritually contend with all false
religions and false ideologies. I will also pray
for the peace of Jerusalem and pray that all
of Israel will be saved (see Mark 11:17).

I want to be a history maker! That is the goal of my life. In fact,
I want you to arise to your priestly and prophetic destiny and help
me and hundreds of thousands of others shape history before the

throne of Almighty God! Are you ready to make a difference? The recipe for enduring change is simple. It is spelled P-R-A-Y! Yes, prayer changes things, and history belongs to the intercessor! That is why effective, fervent intercession is one of the core values of our collective Reformer's Pledge.

Let's arise and get on with God's original program of extending the rod of His Kingdom authority into every cultural sphere of life. Let's impact the seven societal mountains with history-making prayer. It's time to shake us free from the pervasive influence of this lethargic "what will be will be" attitude and take our rightful position seated with Christ Jesus in the heavenly places looking down upon the affairs of humanity. In fact, let's change this present darkness by calling forth brilliant displays of God's great presence. Ready to do it? Let's take the intercession plunge together!

Why do I burn with this message? I burn because this is not just about being highly gifted. Prayer is God's equal opportunity card that each believer in Christ gets to punch! We can each cast out demons! We can each pray for the sick and see them recover, and we can each release history-making intercession! Let's shift things through the prevailing power of effective intercession.

WHAT IS INTERCESSION?

Let's cover some basic points to make sure our foundation is sure. Somebody who intercedes intervenes in a situation, stepping between two parties with the intention of reconciling differences. An intercessor is a "go-between." An intercessor mediates, occupying a middle position. You become a middleman for God! The most familiar phrase is "standing in the gap," which comes from Ezekiel 22:30: *"I [God] sought for a man among them, that should make up the hedge, and stand in the gap before Me for the land, that I should not destroy it: but I found none"* (KJV).

In my book, *The Prophetic Intercessor,* I define intercession as follows:

> The act of making a request to a superior, or express-
> ing a deep-seated yearning to our one and only supe-
> rior, God.

I followed that with a definition of intercessor:

> One who reminds God of His promises and appoint-
> ments yet to be fulfilled; who takes up a case of injus-
> tice before God on behalf of another; who makes up
> the "hedge" (that is, builds up the wall in time of bat-
> tle); and who stands in the gap between God's righ-
> teous judgments and the people's need for mercy.[1]

Jesus, our High Priest, who sacrificed His own life to redeem us from death, is the foremost intercessor. He interposed Himself between sinful humans and the justified wrath of His Father, and He still intercedes for us day and night. We read in the book of Hebrews:

> *Therefore He is able also to save forever those who
> draw near to God through Him, since He always lives
> to make intercession for them* (Hebrews 7:25 NASB).

All believers are called to be intercessors. There is no special list anywhere in the Scriptures indicating that prayer, praise, worship, and intercession are special "gifts of the Holy Spirit." They are the birthright of every believer! We are each called to co-labor with Jesus Christ. We simply lift up to our Father every need, every desire, and every thought. But we do it from the expectant heart, and we do it with a sense of delight, not obligation.

The Bible is filled with urgent summons to pray. *"Rejoice always; pray without ceasing; in everything give thanks; for this is God's will for you in Christ Jesus"* (1 Thess. 5:16-18 NASB). What is God's will? Rejoice, pray, and give thanks at all times! Awesome! What an approachable Father God we have!

FIVE DISTINCT PICTURES OF INTERCESSION

Life begins in intimacy. Communion with God is the bedchamber of the Holy Spirit. But *intercession* is more than just another word for prayer. *Intercession* is defined as "the act of pleading by one who in God's sight has a right to do so in order to obtain mercy for one in need."[2] Perhaps a little word study will help us better understand this concept.

The basic Hebrew word for intercession is *paga,* which is found 44 times in the Old Testament. Although it is translated as "intercession" only a handful of times, *paga,* when we consider all its variations and shades of meaning, gives us a wonderful understanding of what it means to intercede.

1. *Paga* means "to meet," as in meeting with God for the purpose of reconciliation.

   Thou meetest him who rejoiceth and worketh righteousness... (Isaiah 64:5 KJV).

   Intercession creates a meeting between two parties.

2. *Paga* means "to light upon."

And he [Jacob] lighted upon a certain place, and tarried there all night... (Genesis 28:11 KJV).

That night that place became one of divine visitation for Jacob. By God's working of grace, our divine Helper stands by, ready to aid us in our intercession, moving us from the natural to the supernatural and from finite ability to infinite ability, taking hold of situations with us to accomplish the will of God.

3. *Paga* means "to fall upon, attack, strike down, cut down."

   And David called one of the young men, and said, "Go near, and fall upon him." And he smote him that he died (2 Samuel 1:15 KJV).

   Intercession is the readiness of a soldier to fall upon or attack the enemy at the command of his Lord, striking and cutting him down!

4. *Paga* means "to strike the mark."

   He covers His hands with the lightning, and commands it to strike the mark (Job 36:32 NASB).

   Intercession, therefore, releases the glory of God to flash forth into a desired situation and "strike the mark" with His brilliant presence.

5. *Paga* means "to lay upon."

> *...The Lord hath laid on Him the iniquity of us all* (Isaiah 53:6 KJV).
>
> *...He bare the sin of many, and made intercession for the transgressors* (Isaiah 53:12 KJV).
>
> Intercession reached its fullest and most profound expression when our sins were "laid upon" Jesus. Jesus fully identified with us when the totality of all our sins for generations past, present, and future were placed on Him. Then, as the scapegoat, He carried them far away (see Lev. 16:8-10;20-22).[3]

In "burden-bearing intercession" we pick up the burdens of others; we deposit them before the throne of mercy to obtain help for a time of need. We do not keep these burdens; we release them to our gracious, loving Father. In devotional prayer, I bring my adoration and personal needs before my God. But in intercession, we bring our petitions to a loving God in behalf of others.

IN THE FOOTSTEPS OF ABRAHAM

One of the first great intercessors in the Bible was Abraham, and his most famous intercessory prayer was for one of the most sinful places in the ancient world! Sodom and Gomorrah have become synonymous with sin, sexual debauchery, and sodomy, yet the great patriarch of Israel, the "father of faith," interceded passionately that those twin cities of sin be spared! I believe it was this kind of compassion that led God to say, *"Shall I hide from Abraham what I am about to do?"* (Gen. 18:17 NASB).

When God told Abraham that He planned to destroy Sodom and Gomorrah, the patriarch asked God if He planned to destroy the righteous people along with the wicked. Abraham then made the counterproposal, *"...Will You indeed sweep it away and not spare the place for the sake of the fifty righteous who are in it?"* (Gen. 18:24b NASB). When God agreed to relent if 50 righteous people were found, Abraham persisted to drive the numbers lower, knowing that only Lot and his family could possibly qualify. The patriarch whittled the number down to 20, and in verse 32 he reached a pivotal place that is important for us to see. Abraham said, *"Oh may the Lord not be angry, and I shall speak only this once; suppose ten are found there?..."* (Gen. 18:32 NASB).

God agreed to Abraham's request, but this passage causes us to wonder, *What if Abraham hadn't stopped at ten?* God definitely showed no signs of being angry with Abraham over his persistent intercession and pleading on behalf of Sodom and Gomorrah. In fact, I believe God liked it. I have a hunch that Abraham could have gone even lower. (But then again, I wasn't there, and I certainly don't have all the facts at hand.) However, this incident illustrates one of the fundamental laws governing the relationship between God and people: God quits when people quit.

What did you say, James? Yes, God quits when people quit! God loves a good fight, and He calls us to be His tenacious bulldogs in the Holy Spirit—to get hold of the promises of God and not let go until something happens. History-making intercessors just flat out never give up. They continue *until!* I love it... So will you.

FOUR BIBLICAL DEFINITIONS

Four biblical definitions of an intercessor, which I have used over the years to help paint a clear picture of our amazing calling as effective intercessors, will bring everything else we study into proper perspective. But the picture is not complete unless we bring all four of these definitions together. So hold on; you need to get the whole picture, not just a one frame shot. So let's bring some greater definition.

An intercessor is one who:

1. Reminds the Lord of promises and appointments not yet met and fulfilled.

   > *On your walls, O Jerusalem, I have appointed watchmen; All day and all night they will never keep silent.* **You who remind the Lord,** *take no rest for yourselves; and give Him no rest until He establishes and makes Jerusalem a praise in the earth* (Isaiah 62:6-7 NASB).

2. Takes up the case of justice before God on behalf of another.

   > *Yes, truth is lacking; and he who turns aside from evil makes himself a prey. Now the Lord saw, and it was displeasing in His sight that* **there was no justice.** *And He saw that there was no man, and was astonished that there was no one to intercede* (Isaiah 59:15-16a NASB).

3. Builds up the wall of protection against the demonic enemy forces in time of battle.

   > *O Israel, your prophets have been like foxes among ruins. You have not gone up into*

*the breaches, nor did you **build the wall** around the house of Israel to **stand in the battle** on the day of the Lord* (Ezekiel 13:4-5 NASB).

4. Stands in the gap between God's righteous judgment, which is due, and the need for mercy on the people's behalf.

*"And I searched for a man among them who should build up the wall and **stand in the gap before Me** for the land, that I should not destroy it; but I found no one. Thus I have poured out My indignation on them; I have consumed them with the fire of My wrath; their way I have brought upon their heads," declares the Lord God* (Ezekiel 22:30-31 NASB).

Bringing all four of these definitions together, we see that an intercessor is one who relentlessly reminds the Lord of His prophetic promises while identifying the needs for justice in our generation. We do spiritual warfare against the powers of darkness in Jesus' great name while lifting a cry for mercy upon our spheres of delegated rule for Christ name sake! Whew! That is history making for sure. It makes me want to sign up all over again.

RESPONDING TO HIS PROMISES

History-making intercessors deal with two kinds of promises, the promises recorded in the Word of God, which are yet to be fulfilled or are ongoing promises available to every believer by faith, and the prophetic, revelatory promises given to us in our day through the voice of God and the gifts of the Holy Spirit, which are true, but also are yet to be fulfilled (see 1 Tim. 1:18-19). We must contend for the promise!

God tells us in the Book of Jeremiah that He is watching over His Word to perform it (see Jer. 1:12). That means that the most valid and effective way to present our case before God is to rehearse and respectfully remind Him of His unchanging Word. When we rehearse a promise from our faithful God, He requires Himself to watch over that Word to perform it. But this entreaty only can be done with the purest of motives from hearts that are clean before God. Even then, we are only authorized to "argue" or present our case for those things and petitions that (1) are in accordance with God's will, (2) extend His Kingdom, and (3) glorify His name.

Christians who believe in the current-day operation of the gifts of the Spirit need to make sure their arsenal includes one of the foundational evangelical truths, the integrity of the Scriptures as the inspired, infallible Word of God and the final authority in salvation, doctrine, conduct, reproof, and correction. Many evangelicals, on the other hand, need to add the fervor, faith, and power of the present-day ministry of the Holy Spirit.

We need a wedding between the school of the Word and the school of the Spirit. Then and only then can we proceed with assurance into the fullness of what God has in mind for this generation. Years ago, I once publically heard the famous revivalist and statesman Leonard Ravenhill declare, "If you have the Word without the Spirit, you will dry up. If you have the Spirit without the Word, you will blow up. But if you have the Spirit with the Word, you will grow up." I say *amen* to this simple declaration.

So let's kneel on the promises both written and revelatory and birth them from the revelatory, spiritual realm into the natural, earthly realm. Kingdom come! Will be done! On earth as it is in

Heaven! Impose the heavenly rule of Christ Jesus in a time-and-space world. Stretch forth your rod of authority and reign.

THE WHEN AND WHERE OF INTERCESSION

There is a great diversity of style and application that exists in history-making intercession. I have launched an emphasis on "the hour that changes the world" through our GPS (Global Prayer Storm), which is based in people's homes and churches around the globe and networked through the worldwide web. Others emphasize the prayer room or house of prayer approach, as my friend and colleague Mike Bickle does with the influential International House of Prayer (IHOP) based in Kansas City, Missouri.

My friends, who are also healing apostles, Mahesh and Bonnie Chavda with All Nations Church in Fort Mills, South Carolina, have hosted all night prayer watches for years. Pastor David Yonggi Cho, in South Korea, has maintained Prayer Mountain for decades with people praying and fasting in small cubicles. Or consider Tom Hess on the Mount of Olives in Jerusalem, Israel, who calls forth intercession for the 12 Gates of the City. Lou Engle, with TheCall, has hosted massive prayer and fasting rallies in the nations of the earth for crisis intervention and revival.

There are many other diverse and appropriate applications of intercession for the global prayer army to engage in. The consortium of ministries today varies in approach from governmental intercession to soaking prayer centers, from the fire furnaces accentuating young adult involvement to meetings with a missions and revival prayer focus. There is a lot of work that needs to be done, and God uses people with different bents, burdens, and gifts for the many different tasks. Whatever the case, let's just cooperate together and invade the seven cultural mountains for Jesus Christ sake!

THE THREE STATIONS
OF THE WATCHMEN

From the Scriptures we have discussed, it is obvious that God wants to clue us in on His plans and prophetic promises and tip us off concerning the enemy's schemes. But as watchmen on the walls, we can each have a different vantage point according to what position we hold on the wall. Our perspective depends on our position.

I have walked the wall surrounding the Old City of Jerusalem. Each section stands at a different height with a specific lookout point and overlooks a different sector of the city. In this complex maze of religious and architectural wonders, you can see entirely different views of the city. It all depends on your position on the wall.

It is the same for us as we are getting our read in the Holy Spirit. There are many different angles from which we gain our view. Or to change the metaphor, each of us brings a piece of the jigsaw puzzle of God, and when the pieces are brought together, we can see the whole.

There are three biblical positions of the watchmen. They each have a different vantage point and each are needed. These are positioned (1) on the walls of the city (see Isa. 62:6-7), (2) walking about in the city (see Song of Sol. 3:3), and (3) on the hills or in the countryside (see Jer. 31:6). Together these can give us a good picture of the operation of the watchman's ministry.

The Lord Himself has called spiritual watchmen today who are to serve in each of these three diverse positions. He has some whose primary purpose is to be watching within the Church or prayer room for the movement of the King and to make a way for Him. These watchmen are also called to recognize and report to the elders who sit at the gates of the city any demonic activity they see approaching. Thus we see the necessity of intercessors and pastoral leaders working together.

There are also some who have been given a place of vision that enables them to see both inside and outside of the Church world. Other watchmen are called mainly to roam around as field scouts in the world, able to spot such things as the rise of a new cult, political wrong maneuvering, injustices in the earth, or a major persecution against the Church. Just find your assignment and get on with it for Christ sake! We will all win that way.

In the midst of all the diversity and individual callings, there yet remain times where a clear sound is heard and we must all rally to that sound as in Nehemiah's day. The first Thursday in May with the National Day of Prayer, the Global Day of Prayer movement birthed out of South Africa, and the Day to Prayer for the Peace of Jerusalem are examples of calls to prayer that should supersede our own individual goals and callings. We need to all get on board and respond to these calls for the common good.

THE CORPORATE HOUR OF PRAYER

Acts 3:1 tells us there were set hours of corporate prayer in the early Church: *"Peter and John were going up to the temple at the ninth hour, the hour of prayer"* (NASB). When 3:00 P.M. rolled around, Peter and John knew they could get in on a prayer meeting so they joined the other believers in this corporate hour of prayer. It was common knowledge and the practice of the first century Church.

Imagine how tremendous it would be if you went to visit another city and knew that at a certain hour there would be a public time of intercession. No matter what part of the country you were visiting, you could locate the believers in that city and know you could get in on a prayer meeting.

May this, too, be restored in our churches and cities.

THREE TIMES A DAY

Late in the summer or early in the fall, you can hear some serious grunting and groaning going on all across the United States. What is this strange sound? I hear it coming from young people—teenage guys, in fact, at football practice mornings, afternoons, and sometimes even evenings. "No pain, no gain," they say. "The team that sweats together stays together"—or something like that.

Others have released the sounds of agony more than once a day, too—God's intercessory army throughout the generations. King David depicts this model for us in Psalm 55:16-17, which is an inspiration for many modern-day churches and ministries:

> *As for me, I shall call upon God, and the Lord will save me. Evening and morning and at noon, I will complain and murmur, and He will hear my voice* (Psalm 55:16-17 NASB).

The prophet Daniel was one who helped pioneer this model when he, too, lifted his voice three times daily:

> *...[Daniel] entered his house (now in his roof chamber he had windows open toward Jerusalem); and he continued kneeling on his knees three times a day, praying and giving thanks before his God, as he had been doing previously* (Daniel 6:10 NASB).

Morning, noon, and evening, the sacrifices of prayer and praise and the sounds of deliverance are to ascend to the Lord. What a blessing! May our Captain hear the sounds of many more "practices" as the intercessory army grows in strength and numbers from shore to shore. Remember, the team that sweats together....

PRAYING ON-SITE WITH INSIGHT

Among the old implements that have been used in the past to help bring God's people into their promised land is on-site locational prayer. Recall for a moment, the children of Israel circling the city of Jericho.

Across the globe, God is stirring ordinary believers to pray persistently while walking their cities street by street. Some of these prayer warriors use prearranged strategies. Others tend to be more prophetic or spontaneous. Some of these prophetic intercessors make wide-ranging appeals while others pinpoint their petitions like smart bombs for accurate delivery.

Prayer targets vary in distance just as targets in military action do. Some prayer weapons focus on far-reaching points way beyond the intercessors' own homes or neighborhoods. It is hard to stop at your street so most of these marching prayer commandos eventually burst into prayers for their entire campus, city, or even nation.

No quick fix is envisioned among these street warriors. Most of these victorious intercessors do not imagine themselves just holding flickering candles against an overwhelming darkness. Rather, they light long fuses in anticipation of major explosions of God's love being set off around the globe. Expectancy seems to expand with every mile as they lob prayer and praise bombs that are often coupled with practical acts of kindness in Christ's name.

We need many more such combination efforts for Jesus Christ sake. Yes, let's try prayer evangelism!

PRACTICAL POINTERS FOR ON-SITE PRAYING

As one who has done this for years, let me give you a few pointers. This is not a new approach to an old concept. It is an ancient approach, but with fresh applications for our day, and it is happening all around the world. Let me clarify the concept of on-site locational prayer for a brief moment with the following simple points:

1. It is directed intercession. A target is painted and research is done on the purposes for which the city was founded, major wars or battles fought, any destiny declared by the founding fathers, offenses and sins committed, and so forth.

2. It is intentional prayer for a preset period of time.

3. It is on-site intercession in the very places those prayers are expected to be answered.

4. It is prayer with insight. Research and geographical identification are combined with dependence on the Holy Spirit's guidance. The gifts of the Spirit are employed, and revelatory insight with wisdom is sought.

5. It is a refreshment, but not a replacement, for normal in-house prayer meetings.

Today, in many of our neighborhoods, you can find signs posted stating, *This is a Neighborhood Watch area.* In other words, citizens are watching out particularly at nighttime for their residential area to be safe and secure. They are looking out for one another. Wouldn't it be great to have a whole city under the watch of the Holy Spirit? As this form of praying on site with insight grows, maybe we will have entire cities canvassed by prayer walkers. Signs could then be put up that say, *This city is under spiritual surveillance.* Awesome!

May the watchmen come forth, taking their positions on the walls.

APPOINTED A WATCHMAN FOR ISRAEL

Before I close out this strategic chapter as a part of our Reformer's Pledge, I have to address a subject that is dear to the heart of God. It deals with God's heart for a specific plot of ground in the middle of the earth and a particular covenant people—Israel. An appointment awaits you.

As stated earlier, watchmen have a task of reminding God of His appointments on His calendar, which have not fully been met and fulfilled. The task of watchmen is by "appointment." It means you are chosen for the divine privilege of composing history before the throne of the Almighty.

SCRIPTURAL REASONS WHY
I PRAY FOR ISRAEL

Let me give you some Scriptural reasons why I pray and take a stand for Israel. This is a short clip that I hope will help bring the big picture into focus. For a complete overview of this subject, see my book *Praying for Israel's Destiny*.[4]

> 1. Pray for and take a stand for Israel because Israel is still very close to God's heart. Zechariah 2:8 states, *"...for he who touches you* [Israel], *touches the apple of His eye"* (NASB). Some other translations render the phrase *apple of God's eye* as "the pupil of God's eye." Centuries before this text was composed, Moses wrote a song containing a very similar picture:

For the Lord's portion is His people; Jacob [Israel] is the allotment of His inheritance....He encircled him, He cared for him, He guarded him as the pupil of His eye....He spread His wings and caught them, He carried them on His pinions (Deuteronomy 32:9-11 NASB).

And he has lifted up a horn for His people, praise for all His godly ones; even for the sons of Israel, a people near to Him... (Psalm 148:14 NASB).

Did you hear that? *A people near to Him.* I love that.

The first reason why I pray for Israel is simple, not profound. I pray for Israel because I want to be close to God's heart, and I want to be in alignment with God's sight. If God says that Israel is the apple or pupil of His eye, then I want to pray with insight with His sight. Do you want to be close to the heart of God? Then be close to the things, people, and purposes that are close to His heart.

2. Pray and take a stand for Israel because God wants to establish Jerusalem and make her a praise in the earth. The prophet Isaiah declared the following:

   On your walls, O Jerusalem, I have appointed watchmen; all day and all night they will never keep silent. You who remind the Lord, take no rest for yourselves;

and give Him no rest until He establishes and makes Jerusalem a praise in the earth (Isaiah 62:6-7 NASB).

Give Him no rest until what? Jerusalem is established! He didn't say Washington D.C., Paris, or London. He didn't say Constantinople, Athens, Hong Kong, Damascus, Moscow, or Cairo. He said until *Jerusalem* is made a *praise.* Many news reports will tell you that Jerusalem seems to be far from being a praise in the earth. Many curse Jerusalem and call the Jewish people names I will not even dare restate. So we must lift our voices in prayer until she becomes a praise—a glorious praise—in all the earth.

3. Pray and act for Israel so that Israel will be saved. I have shared that God wants to give us His heart of compassion for Israel. God desires that we receive His heart so that He can pray with accuracy and discernment for the salvation of Israel. The apostle Paul said:

I have great sorrow and unceasing grief in my heart.... My heart's desire and my prayer to God for them is for their salvation (Romans 9:2; 10:1).

Paul further declared, *"I could wish that I myself were accursed...for the sake of my brethren...who are Israelites..."* (Rom. 9:3-4 NASB).

I have prayed this verse from the book of Romans many times. I have fasted and wept much over the years for Israel's sake. We must pray for

Israel's salvation to go forth like a torch that is burning. God has desires…the apostle Paul had desires…do you pray with a burning heart of desire for Israel's salvation?

4. Pray and act for Israel because the Jewish people's acceptance of the Messiah Jesus will lead to worldwide revival of unprecedented magnitude.

> *For if* [Israel's] *rejection [of Christ] be the reconciliation of the world, what will their acceptance be but life from the dead?* (Romans 11:15)

Wow! Life from the dead!

Isaiah prophesied, *"In the days to come Jacob will take root, Israel will blossom and sprout, and they will fill the whole earth with fruit"* (Isa. 27:6 NASB).

One of the major keys to world revival is praying for Israel. As the Jewish people are awakened out of their sleep and behold their Messiah, it will create a divine acceleration into a time when hundreds of thousands, if not literally millions, turn to Jesus as their Messiah. There is nothing more potent than a Jewish believer in the Messiah telling others about the God of Abraham, Isaac, and Jacob. Want to see worldwide revival? Then pray!

5. Pray and take a stand for Israel because the Second Coming of Christ is linked to Israel's response to Him.

Jesus prophesied before His death:

> *For I say to you, from now on you shall not see Me until you say, "Blessed is He who comes in the name of the Lord"* (Matthew 23:39 NASB).

Jesus linked His Second Coming to Israel's national returning or turning to Him.

Do you want to see Jesus come back in your lifetime? Is it possible to hasten the day of His appearing? (See 2 Peter 3:12.) Do you want to see Jesus come again? If so, pray that the blinders on the Jewish people's eyes will fall off (see Rom. 11:25) and that they will welcome their Messiah with a whole heart.

Why should we pray and take a stand of action for Israel? Jesus said to, Isaiah said to, David the psalmist said to, and today the Holy Spirit is saying to.

AS THE WATERS COVER THE SEA

God has clearly portrayed in His Word His desire and intention to bring revival to His people and spiritual awakening to the earth. His promise is straightforward:

> *For the earth shall be filled with the knowledge of the glory of the Lord, as the waters cover the sea* (Habakkuk 2:14 KJV).

A day is coming when the knowledge of the glory of the Lord will fill the earth. In that end-time season, all people will see Him and, willingly or not, acknowledge His presence and His glory. Christ will be magnified and glorified in His Church, and His name will be exalted above every other name so that every knee will bow and every tongue confess that He is Lord, to the glory of God the Father (see Phil. 2:9-11). All things will be put in subjection under Christ's feet; He then will subject Himself to the Father in order that *"God may be all in all"* (1 Cor. 15:27-28 NASB).

Are there keys to unlocking the glory of God? Yes, the Scriptures are full of them. Consider the following passage:

> *You shall make an altar of earth for Me, and you shall sacrifice on it your burnt offerings and your peace offerings, your sheep and your oxen; in every place where I cause My name to be remembered, I will come to you and bless you* (Exodus 20:24 NASB).

Where will God's name be "remembered"? Everywhere an altar is built. In fact, the whole earth is to be offered up as an altar where the fire shall be kept burning and never go out (see Lev. 6:9-13). Are you building an altar of worship, praise, prayer, and intercession?

WANT YOUR LIFE TO MAKE A DIFFERENCE?

I am not satisfied with reading about history. I want to live it! Do you want your life to make a difference? Then join me and throngs of others who are history-making intercessors. Remember, time spent with God is not time wasted—it is time gained!

Here is my goal. I want to be a battering ram for the Lord that can break through doors that have been shut and bust wide open low ceilings of limitation through the passion and power of intercession.

I exhort you to get so saturated by the presence of Jesus that you will carry an open Heaven over your own head. Then wherever you go, you will create an atmospheric change by becoming a "gate of Heaven" for others.

Does that seem like a hard task? It's not if you know and practice the passion and the power of intercession! Do you want to shape history? Follow along with me on the path well worn by pilgrims of former days; let's shake this generation for Jesus Christ sake!

> *Father, I present myself to you for the purpose of prayer. I join the host of others who are praying around the world at this time. Come, Holy Spirit, and take possession of us all. Fill me with the Spirit of grace and supplication in Jesus' name and for the sake of Your Kingdom. I volunteer freely in the day of Your power to be a watchman on the walls for such a time as this. Amen.*

Chapter 4

GOING FROM GLORY TO GLORY

BILL JOHNSON

Pledge 4: **I will contend for revival in the
Church and spiritual awakening in my nation,
and I will continually be filled with the
power of the Holy Spirit (see Joel 2:28).**

It is a great honor to be alive at a time when the world is in such crisis. The answers to the issues raised by this state of crisis belong to the Church. To you it has been granted to know the mysteries of the Kingdom of Heaven (see Matt. 13:11). But these truths are hidden—hidden *for* us, not *from* us. *...It is the glory of God to conceal a matter, but the glory of kings is to search out a matter* (Prov. 25:2).

The heavenly realm contains all the answers to the problems of this world.

Perhaps the greatest commission of all is our assignment to pray. Jesus specifically revealed the overriding theme of His life in telling us how and what to ask for with the expectation: *"...On earth as it is in heaven"* (Matt. 6:10). That expression in prayer sums up the heart of God for every situation—His world has the answer to this one. The outpouring of the Spirit is on earth as it is in Heaven! God's target is to affect all realms of society through the Holy Spirit. By correctly changing our view of revival, we can be positioned to take the move of God where He alone can take us: to city and national transformation. There must be a time when the earth receives the witness of the fullness of Jesus seen through His people still on the planet. That is our charge—our commission. We must fully step into what Jesus announced when He prophesied, *"greater works than these* [you] *will do"* (John 14:12).

Our identity is clear. We are kings and priests—ambassadors of another world to bring about change. But the change must be done Heaven's way. God's kind of king rules with the heart of a servant for kings who follow the King of kings live to empower others to reach their God-given destiny and purpose. It is also time for us to serve with the heart of a king. For only in serving from this perspective can we access the unlimited resources of Heaven to meet the challenges of the day. *But the path of the righteous is like the light of dawn, that shines brighter and brighter until the full day* (Prov. 4:18 NASB).

DOES HISTORY TEACH US WELL?

Revivals have come and gone. Their fruit is evident. But because every revival was short lived, students of revival tend to come to the conclusion that revivals are supposed to be short spurts of spiritual activity designed to bring strength to the Church for the next season. For far too long our understanding of revivals and reformations has been defined by history instead of by the nature of God. We look at what ended in a previous outpouring and conclude it was supposed to end in that way. The problem I have with this understanding is that human failure contributes to the conclusion. There will come a time when God's nature, person, and presence will actually define the move of God on the earth, which is one of continuous, increasing glory! In the Old Testament it was God who lit the fire on the altar. But it was the priest that kept it burning (see Lev. 6:12-13). Revivals start because of God. They end because of people.

REDEFINING REVIVAL

History provides wonderful stories that set a legal precedent for the minimum of what we can expect in our lifetimes. But as wonderful as these stories are, they are not to confine us. For example, some of the greatest moves of God in history started with such a great conviction of sin that people's hearts were only satisfied when they made public confession. This was true evidence of deep repentance. But when we define revival by that manifestation, we actually need sin to continue in revival! Our understanding must adjust so that we are intentional in enlarging the pursuit, practice, and advancement of revival from the gathering of believers into society itself. We must be careful to follow God when He moves from one manifestation to another. God is after cities and nations. We must adjust our prayers and plans to fit His agenda.

Revivals are sometimes defined by how many meetings a church has during the week. In recent years many have had meetings five to seven nights a week. I personally love when that happens. It is only possible when God has given an unusual grace to a congregation. It's exciting when the people of God want to be together day after day. An amazing momentum is created in that environment that releases a potential transformation of society. But tragically, cities often go unchanged even though the Church is experiencing a genuine move of God. The devil doesn't seem to be threatened by the people of God having a spiritual breakthrough if we keep it within the context of Church-life. It's when the "burning ones" find their place in society that the forces of darkness know they've lost ground. We must redefine revival to include the release of God's people into the systems of society and succeed in establishing true Kingdom culture in its citizens.

No wonder revival has been short lived! If a great move of God is measured by the number of meetings we have per week, it becomes nearly impossible to maintain such a difficult schedule. We have only so much physical and emotional strength. But perhaps the bigger loss is the fact that the ones becoming transformed by such powerful encounters with God are at the same time removed from any practical interaction with unbelievers due to the imposing schedule. The human element is always with us as a boundary that must be respected. As one prophet told me in warning, "The spiritual laws are superior to the natural laws. But failure to keep the natural laws can take you out." The human body can only live under that schedule for so long.

As God comes in power time and time again, leaders need to prepare themselves and their church families with a strategy that includes giving place for the increase of revival fires through frequent gatherings per week, but they also need a plan in place for people to maintain interaction with those in their cities. Permission must be given by those in authority for the people to take care of the other areas of life while in the midst of a great visitation of God.

Another flaw in that definition is that we think the world is supposed to come to us. That in itself is an aberration. While it is certainly amazing and enjoyable when the world beats a path to our door, it is also necessary for our "salt, light, and leaven" to invade the culture of our communities so that the influence of the Kingdom in us redefines the way our cities and nations live (see Matt. 5:14-16;13:33). This kind of transformation sets God's presence and purity in motion in ways that can have an impact on generations we will never see. This is the intended far-reaching effect of an out-pouring of the Spirit.

GOD'S NATURE

When we define revival from an understanding of God's nature instead of ours, we'll be ready for the increase He desires for us. He takes us from glory to glory. *Of the increase of His government and peace there will be no end...* (Isa. 9:7).

His nature is one of continual increase and advance because of His goodness. It is out of that nature that we have been promised that *"all things work together for good"* (Rom. 8:28). It is His commitment to us to make sure that everything we will trust Him for will be used for Kingdom increase in and through us.

Even the lessons of spiritual warfare reinforce this theme of advancement. The spiritual tools mentioned in Ephesians 6 illustrate this beautifully with "the armor of God."

> *For our struggle is not against flesh and blood, but against the rulers, against the powers, against the world forces of this darkness, against the spiritual forces of wickedness in the heavenly places. Therefore, take up the full **armor of God**, so that you will be able to resist in the evil day, and having done every-thing, to stand firm. Stand firm therefore, having girded your loins with truth, and having put on the*

breastplate of righteousness, and having shod your feet with the preparation of the gospel of peace; in addition to all, taking up the shield of faith with which you will be able to extinguish all the flaming arrows of the evil one. And take the helmet of salvation, and the sword of the Spirit, which is the word of God (Ephesians 6:12-17 NASB).

A great truth in this passage is that our armor is not something separate from God Himself. *God is our armor.* It is His righteousness that covers my heart. He is my salvation. As such, He protects my mind. And the list goes on. But please notice that there is no armor for our backs. We have but one focus: forward motion!

DIVINE ORDER AND PURPOSE

It's been said that the purpose of war is victory, and the purpose of victory is occupation. But Jesus takes that principle a bit further than the great generals of history. For Him, the purpose of occupation is always for expansion and advancement. History is filled with those who simply lived to protect what the previous generation had accomplished. But to occupy without the commitment to expand is dangerous. Ask the guy who buried his one talent (see Matt. 25:25-28). He was one of three servants given a sum of money to invest so that his master might obtain a profit. But he was the only one who protected what he was given so he could return it to his master without profit. He was severely judged for *not* using it for increase.

This Kingdom has the nature of its King. This is a Kingdom of increase. And while we experience setbacks, they should never become the focus of our theology. Whatever we build a doctrine around will initially be tolerated and ultimately embraced as God's will for our lives. Whatever we tolerate will, in the end, dominate us. Our theology must be formed around God's nature, not ours. He is good, always. Because these things are true, the safest place in a spiritual war is to be on the front lines of battle. People tend to become increasingly careless the further away from the front lines of battle they get. Figuratively speaking, we're concerned about very little on the front lines—keeping our heads down, having enough ammunition, and knowing where our fellow soldiers are. At the back end of the battle, our focus is different. Trivial matters like the food in the mess hall tent and the movie shown on Friday night become the great concerns. You can tell where a person is in relation to the front lines of battle by the problems he has.

WHAT TRULY HINDERS REVIVAL

I have heard many great sermons through the years on "What is hindering revival." They usually start with statements like, "We can't have revival until…." At this point, the preacher inserts the God-given burden of his heart. For example:

- We'll never have revival until we commit ourselves to lives of prayer.

- Until the Church deals with the issues of true holiness, we will not have a revival.

- If we don't repent for the social ills of abortion and the like that have taken place on our shift, we will never have revival.

- If we don't restore Israel to her rightful place in the eyes of the Church, we'll never have revival.

- If the Church doesn't deal with its materialistic ways and care for the poor, we'll never have revival.

- We must deal with the breakdown of the family or we'll never have revival.

- We must make things right with the First Nations Peoples or we'll never have revival.

This list could go on and on and on. Every issue mentioned *is vital to the Lord and must be attended to.* But are they really prerequisites?

We have given attention to each of these issues and have experienced significant breakthrough in each area of this list. But quite honestly, the outpouring we are experiencing didn't start because we did things right. He came because we were hungry for Him. When God's people deal with the issues of God's heart, it is most often *the fruit of revival,* not the cause. When we mistake them for the cause, the move of God gets removed from grace and put into the category of wages (for correct works). *Every move of God starts in grace because God is in charge.* Tragically, they end with people in charge, often in the barren land of legalism.

THE LETTER KILLS

Any time the fruit is exalted above its rightful place, grace loses its place of defining the move of God. This is something God simply will not bless. Legalism is often taught by people who once had a move of God and try to get it back through legislation. They take things they were inspired to do in an outpouring of the Spirit and make them mandatory in order to get the outpouring back again or even to increase it. The Church of the first century sold their possessions to care for the needy among them. They then gave the proceeds of lands they had sold to the apostles, trusting them to distribute the money as they saw fit. They were not commanded to do this. It was the expression of the overflow of their worship of God. Today we have people taking what the early Church did, as a joyful expression of the work of the Spirit among them, and trying to make it a command in order for us to have the same move of God that the early Church experienced. Although it may be with good intentions, it is the kind of thing that destroys a move of God. He still likes to be in charge in this Kingdom of grace.

It's hard for us to have the same fruit as the early Church when we value a book they didn't have more than we value the Holy Spirit, whom they did have. I don't say that to devalue the Bible. It is the inspired Word of God. It's just that we must reestablish the correct value for the Holy Spirit, who alone can interpret and empower us in the reading and living of the Scriptures. There is a tension between these two realities that the apostle Paul addressed when he said, *"The letter kills, but the Spirit gives life"* (2 Cor. 3:6). It's not either/or. The Spirit makes the Word come alive and enables us to live what we read.

ARCHITECTS OF CULTURE

Several years ago I ministered in a city that is known as the headquarters of a well-known cult. The beliefs of this particular cult are laughable, as I guess they all are. But I felt a conviction in my heart when I drove around that city. It became obvious to me how they had managed to still be around after all these years. They had succeeded in creating a culture to sustain their movement. (A culture is a system of beliefs, practices, relational boundaries, and disciplines.) People who didn't even believe what that cult believed lived under its influence. More importantly, they lived as an expression of that movement.

Through these observations, it became apparent to me that unless we learn how to become architects of a revival culture, we will have a movement that is only short lived, like all the others in history. Something needs to change in our thinking, in our expectations, and in our risk-taking practices.

Several questions must be asked in this regard. What does it look like to have a culture based on the true cornerstones of thought discovered in a great spiritual outpouring? Here are four cornerstones that shape everything we think and do. When these four go beyond doctrines to places of experience and sources of thought, they truly become cultural cornerstones.

1. God is good, always.

2. Nothing is impossible.

3. We fight *from* the victory of Jesus at Calvary, not for it.

4. I am significant.

GROW UP BY GROWING DOWN

Biblical maturity is a bit different than we are sometimes taught. We are to *"become as little children"* (Matt. 18:3). The word *become* means "to come into being." It implies going from one condition to another, as in forward progress. Becoming as children is a step up in Kingdom realities. It is a sign of Kingdom development. In this Kingdom, we give in order to receive and humble ourselves to be exalted (see James 4:10). In the same way, we are to become as children to enter maturity.

Much of what has been called maturity is nothing more than people choosing where they want to level off in their development. By doing so, they take a posture that automatically rejects what God wants to do that is different from what they have already experienced. This might explain why it is almost always the people from the last move of God who reject what God is doing in the next. To them, it is unthinkable that God would do something without them at the center. After all, they were the ones used to advance the last outpouring.

Once we have experienced an outpouring of the Spirit for a season, we start understanding how God moves and how we can work with Him. One of my most frequent prayers is that God would show me how He moves. I want to see more of His movement in the unseen world. And while our understanding should increase the longer we move with God, so should our questions and our dependency on Him. My brother-in-law once told me that the main thing he learned in pursuing his multiple college degrees was how much he didn't know. If only revivalists could be the same.

What we know can keep us from what we need to know if we don't remain novices. We are the most dangerous to a move of God when we go from being like children in the adventure of our lives to being the adult who understands and comprehends what God is doing or, worse yet, what He is going to do. Children have adventure as a core value. They seemingly will try anything. We buy them a wonderful gift and they end up playing with the box. It is sometimes more fun to use their imagination with the box than to do what is expected with the toy. They also only dream of personal significance. And that place of significance is according to what they deem to be important. For example, they might want to be firefighters, police officers, or astronauts. They want to be scientists, nurses, or musicians. By nature children only think in terms of significance. If only children were raised in such a way that they learned how to fulfill dreams.

All 5-year-olds are also artists. Creativity works in tandem with adventure. The willingness—or need—to color outside the lines is an important part of the development of a child's heart. But somehow our educational system decides who really is the artist and who isn't. Without adults who continue to celebrate their accomplishments in the realm of creativity, children put down the paintbrush for something more gratifying to the ones whose opinion they value. This is not to say that every child is to become a Rembrandt or a Michelangelo. But it is to say that full development only happens in any area where creativity is allowed and encouraged.

John and Carol Arnott and Randy and DeAnne Clark are leaders in one of the greatest outpourings of the Spirit of God in the last century. It started at the Toronto Airport Christian Fellowship, where John and Carol are pastors. God used Randy Clark to release the fires of renewal and revival in a way that has impacted almost every nation of the world since its beginning in January of 1994. They are heroes of mine because of the way they have stewarded an extraordinary outpouring of the Holy Spirit. I have watched them for many years as they have maintained the joyful heart of a child at the center of all they are and do. From my personal observation, they are as appreciative now as they were 15 years ago when this outpouring started.

Without these traits, this generation that was born for revival will find it difficult to maintain and advance what God intends to do in the earth. Childlikeness keeps us ready to move on to new things, but also enables us to delight in the simple things already present.

ADJUSTING TO GOD

Everyone enters a revival in ignorance. That is true for many reasons, not the least of which is that every move of God introduces something that is different from what the previous generation experienced. By nature, revivals help to restore what's been lost from the Book of Acts experience. But there is also the additional reality that God almost always adds something to the outpouring that is offensive in the area of manifestations. Getting over hurdles of offense is often the prerequisite to entering Kingdom realities. Our minds must be offended to reveal our hearts. Jesus said, *"The kingdom of God is within you"* (Luke 17:21). All Kingdom issues are heart issues. Heart issues are always His targets in His dealings with His people.

I love to read of the great moves of God throughout history. I am especially thrilled when the author was willing to speak of the things he or she didn't understand. Tragically, accounts of some of the greatest outpourings of the Spirit were watered down by the removal of the record of offensive manifestations by historians who wanted to preserve the memory of a move of God through the filter of their value system. The Shantung revival in China is such an example. Filled with extraordinary experiences and supernatural occurrences in the original records, it was reprinted by a major denomination and stripped of most of the unexplainable things. The *revised* edition is very boring to read.

God told us that He was going to do things that were beyond our comprehension. Even the outpouring of the Spirit in Acts 2 produced these reactions: they were *confused* and *amazed*, they *marveled* and were *perplexed*, and some even *mocked* (see Acts 2:6-13). Those are also fruits of revival. I can't figure out why we have such a tendency to only accept what we can understand and reject everything else. Many seem to want the God who promises to do a new thing among us to do it the way He's always done it. Limiting God has its consequences.

> *Yes, again and again they tempted God, and limited the Holy One of Israel. They did not remember His*

*power: the day when He redeemed them from the
enemy* (Psalm 78:41-42).

To *limit* Him is to *tempt* Him.

PREPARING FOR *MORE!*

There are some things that happen with an "and suddenly," as
the outpouring of the Spirit in Acts 2. But even in that event of all
events, where Heaven invaded earth, "suddenly" followed 10 days of
120 people invading Heaven in prayer. Many things that appear to be
sudden invasions of God are actually Heaven's response to prolonged
faithfulness by believers. Being a good steward of a divine moment
can set you up for dramatic increase and reward. One of the greatest stories of Kingdom stewardship is the one Jesus brought before
His disciples when they expected the Kingdom to come in fullness
at any moment—as in *immediately*. The story is found in Luke 19.
The disciples were interested in the earthly manifestation of Christ's
rule over the earth, which they believed would vindicate the injustices
shown to Israel by surrounding nations. They hoped to sit on the
right and left hand of this wonderful King. In the story Jesus told, a
landowner gave 10 servants 10 minas, which is a sum of money. After
giving them something to work with to make more money, he left the
country. Often, when God has released something to us to steward,
He removes His *recognized* presence so that we can learn faithfulness in ministry apart from the emotional rush that comes from Him
being with us. The landowner then returns to collect the profits from
his servants. The first one comes to him with 10 additional minas.
The master is very impressed and makes his servant the governor over
a region of 10 cities. Think about it. From being faithful in the use of
10 minas to having influence over 10 cities is quite a dramatic promotion. Prolonged obedience is rewarded in a dramatic way.

The disciples were given a story about the importance of steward-ship. It's not that there aren't sudden invasions of God. There are. But they usually follow faithful stewardship from His people. Servants who were good stewards over what their master had put into their care could accomplish their desire for worldwide influence for Christ. Serving well (using minas correctly) released them to a great place of influence (ruling over 10 cities). It's no different today.

THE POWER OF INHERITANCE

If there's never been a revival that has increased in momentum and power in the second generation, then we must conclude that every revivalist was spiritually fatherless as it pertains to revival. The sobering reality is that the world has never seen what a move of God would look like if it was taken where no one generation had time to take it. What could happen if the unity of generations was entirely devoted to a revival that spread over a 100-year period of time with continuous increase? To make this shift, we must learn the power of inheritance.

An inheritance is when I get something for free that someone else paid a price for. But if I'm going to leave something to those who follow me, I'll have to pay a price to increase what I got for free. This is the nature of inheritance. It is as true in the spiritual as it is in the natural.

As they would be with wealth, a generation must be taught the value of what they've been given spiritually. Without this value, they will almost certainly disregard their moment in history. Some of the royal families of the past serve as good examples here. Their chil-dren grew up knowing that their purpose in life was an uncommon privilege. At an early age their appetites were shaped to sustain the "royalty" of their family line. A generation of revivalists must be trained the same way.

The new priests must be taught how to keep fire on the altar by understanding and practicing what it means to be a living sacrifice. They must be given permission to go beyond protecting what we've given to them; they must be released to increase and expand it. It is the only honorable way to live.

THE ATMOSPHERE OF INCREASE

The wonderful story of Jesus multiplying food gives us another great revelation on the Kingdom. Jesus started with only a few loaves and fishes. But *after* He gave thanks for little, it became much. Thankfulness is the atmosphere of great increase. If it is hard for us to recognize and be thankful for the slightest glimpses of revival, we will not likely be entrusted with the full manifestation.

When my wife and I became the pastors of Bethel Church in Redding, California, we came with the sole commitment to see a great move of God. Our church in the small mountain community of Weaverville, California, was experiencing a wonderful outpouring of the Spirit. The mother church (Bethel), asked us to come back to Redding for the purpose of spreading the outpouring that we were having in Weaverville.

On one of the first Sunday nights, I asked the whole church to come to the front to pray. Hundreds crowded around the front of the sanctuary in excited anticipation. I invited the Holy Spirit to come in power, and He fell powerfully on one person. My wife, Beni, and I looked at each other like we had just won the big sweepstakes. Despite the fact that only one person was impacted powerfully by God's touch, we knew that this move of God was now unstoppable, and we gave thanks accordingly.

Many have experienced the same, but walked away disappointed because there wasn't a large group of people affected by this "initial lightning strike." We make a serious mistake when we judge an outpouring by the number of people affected. What God does is not to be defined by what people do. We treated this outpouring as the greatest possible thing to be entrusted with by God. By honoring God for this move of the Spirit and by treating this move with the utmost care and value (*before* it got big), we positioned ourselves for the more that everyone wants.

If I pick a fully ripe apple off of a tree and then pick one that has just begun to grow, unfair comparisons are easy. Yet they are both 100 percent apple. Sometimes failing to recognize what we have is the block to thankfulness. And thankfulness is the atmosphere that brings increase. If I don't carry the attitude of gratitude, I will unintentionally dishonor the Holy Spirit by not recognizing that the Spirit of God has fallen upon us.

A number of years ago, I flew to Argentina to join Randy Clark. I had read of the revival that they had been experiencing for many years. I wanted to go there to find out whether my assessment of our experience warranted the label "revival." It didn't take long to recognize that we had the "small apple," but it was still 100 percent apple. There's no way in the world that I was going to dishonor what God had given me because of my desire for more. Those things (a full-blown revival that brings citywide and nationwide transformation) come as we steward what we've been given.

My dad's mom died many years ago at the age of 97. But before she died, my dad, my brother, my brother-in-law, and I went to visit her. Besides the obvious desire to spend time with her, I wanted to find out how the outpouring of the Spirit that we were experiencing compared to what she had seen in the Pentecostal outpouring of the early 1900s. She told us wonderful stories. Then she asked me about what we were seeing. When I was through, she said, "Oh, then you have more than we did." It would be easy to exalt history above the present and miss the significance of the moment.

So much of what we come into is obtained by faith. Is it possible that we should have a faith in God's Word that He will actually take us from glory to glory? After all, we have been entrusted with the original flame. It doesn't honor our forefathers to value their breakthroughs so much that we fail to build upon them and to actually go where they didn't have time to go.

USING OUR LOSSES

It is easy to be one of the burning ones for God when the miracles are on the right hand and the left. One of the greatest honors in life is to see God use us for things that are far beyond our reach. But it's quite another to know how to advance in the face of loss and disappointment. In fact, I don't think it's possible for us to fully come into our destiny until we have learned this very important lesson.

This is done first by escaping the temptation of blaming God for our loss. I have found it useful to give God honor for the very thing in question. For example, if it appears that God didn't keep His promise to you, loudly celebrate His faithfulness to keep His Word. We know the problem is never with God. So respond to Him accordingly.

It's hard to have the peace that passes understanding if I don't give up my right to understand. Not holding God hostage to an explanation is huge for many of us. It's not that God doesn't want to give us understanding. It's just that we need to lay it down as a right, and celebrate His goodness…sometimes entirely from a place of faith. Too many people only do what they feel like doing, thinking that it is hypocrisy to do what they don't feel like doing. It's the opposite for the believer. It's hypocritical to do only what I feel like doing. I've learned that for Kingdom minded people, we do things because they are right, and the feeling follows.

From that place of peace comes the biggest step of increase— Divine Justice. This is when, through true surrender of our loss and disappointment, we place that experience as a seed into the ground of His care. He alone can make it bear fruit. He is able to bring about His justice so that the very area of loss becomes our place of greatest triumph. God is able to bring a seven times greater breakthrough into our lives through that loss if it is yielded to Him.

THE PRIORITY OF HIS PRESENCE

Yesterday's anointing is like yesterday's manna. Keeping current with God is more important now than it was for Israel in the wilderness. And for them it was life and death. Greater anointings often come from greater encounters with the Anointed One. Pursuing more, while honoring the present, is the tightrope we've been called to walk.

The presence of God is the greatest treasure of true revivalists. We have nothing without Him. It is fairly easy to try to live by these principles of increase, yet never touch what God has planned for us. The bottom line is that we are not dealing with a business, a social enterprise, or a personal goal. We have been given a treasure: God Himself. And learning to live from His presence, not just Kingdom principles, is what will take us where we want to go. We will not go further by great strategy and better government. The wine is the treasure, not the wineskin. All structure is to give passion a place, while strategy is to give passion a focus.

The New Jerusalem, the four square city that comes down from Heaven as a bride in Revelation 19, illustrates this perfectly. The city is the emblem of perfect structure. But as the bride, it tells me that heavenly structure is formed in romance.

Experts have examined the effect of influential people on their surroundings. They found that if you have a meeting with a small group of people, the person with the greatest influence will actually affect the heart rate and the emotional condition of the others in the room. This is true even if that person is not the one with the greatest authority or the most significant title.[1]

When the presence of God is really the greatest influence in the room, the heart of God will affect the heartbeat of everyone else in the room. Our hearts will beat as one! Maybe this is another way of saying, *"I only do what I see my Father doing"* (John 5:19). It is the manifest presence of God that is truly our greatest treasure. And that becomes a reality as He takes us continually from glory to glory.

Chapter 5

CREATING A CULTURE OF LIFE

LOU ENGLE

Pledge 5: I will contend for the rights of the unborn until abortion is illegal and rare. I will not vote for anyone who is pro-choice (see Exod. 20:1).

"I'm a murderer, I'm a murderer!" Her cry of confession shocked me as a college student. It was shortly after the legalization of abortion in 1973, but abortion was totally off my radar. I could not comprehend the young lady's soul-stabbing wounded conscience as she told me she had had an abortion. As I look back, I know now that God was preparing me for the call that I would receive from Heaven in 2003.

Flying home from Canada, while reading the book *Wilberforce: The Nation's Conscience* by Patrick Cormack, I was suddenly pierced by the fiery quote of the great British abolitionist Thomas Clarkson:

I urged myself that never was any cause, which had been taken up by man in any country or in any age, so great and important; never was there one, in which so much good could be done; never one in which the duty of Christian charity could be so extensively exercised; never one, more worthy of devotion of a whole life towards it; and that, if a man thought properly, he ought to rejoice to have been called into existence, if he were only permitted to become an instrument in forwarding it in any part of its progress.[1]

As I finished reading this man's resolve to give his life for the cause of the abolition of slavery, the Spirit of God forcefully apprehended my heart with an undeniable and irrevocable commission, *"Raise up a prayer movement to end abortion in America."* Trying to hide the weeping that swept over me, I resolved to dedicate my life to the great cause—the ending of abortion and the creation of a culture of life.

John Noonan, professor at UC Berkeley, stated:

Once or twice in a century an issue arises...so far reaching in its consequences, and so deep in its foundations that it calls every person to take a stand.[2]

Abortion is one of those issues. Fifty million preborn babies have been aborted in the United States since 1973.[3] As Senator Sam Brownback has said, *"In every abortion there is one killed and one wounded, the baby and the mother."*[4]

Really it's not just those, but also the father, the extended families, and a whole generation who suffer. At the root of the culture of death in America is abortion.

If the Church is going to bring reformation to a nation and create a culture of life out of the ashes and agony of this culture of death, we must first define and align ourselves with the blueprint culture of life that God has laid out in Scripture. All other paradigms are the shifting sands of humanistic reasoning.

SOLA SCRIPTURA

If we want to see abortion ended in our day, the Church must submit her political preferences and rebellious reasoning to the measuring rod of God's truth. God gave us courageous men and women like Martin Luther who challenged the whole religious system of his day and its false ideologies of salvation with the trumpet phrase, *Sola Scriptura*, meaning "Scripture alone." Vast portions of the Church today, ringing with the hollow echo of "relevance," are dumbing down the razor's edge of biblical truth for the sake of acceptance and are following a pattern of apostasy that breaks away from God's fixed moral standards. This tendency is illustrated by postmodern preacher, Rob Bell, who states:

> It wasn't until the 300s that what we know as the sixty-six books of the Bible were actually agreed upon as the 'Bible'. This is part of the problem with continually insisting that one of the absolutes of the Christian faith must be a belief that "Scripture Alone" is our guide. It sounds nice, but it is not true.[5]

This so-called Christian wisdom is training a whole generation in moral relativity. If there are no absolute truths by which we shape our personal convictions and our political opinions, then everything, from the covenant of marriage, to what is taught in our schools, to our sexual boundaries, to our value of human life, can be changed at the whim of a feeling or a difficult circumstance.

Luther, under the threat of death, refused to recant his views before a Papal court and stood as a faithful witness to Christ declaring:

> *Unless I am convinced by proofs from scriptures...*I can and will not retract, for it is neither safe nor wise to do anything against conscience. Here I stand. I can do no other. God help me. Amen.[6]

There must be a new courageous voice of reformation heard in the high schools, universities, and pulpits in our land, resounding with a cry "Sola Scriptura!" Our private lives and our public politics must align with God's culture of life rooted in the Scriptures.

BE FRUITFUL AND MULTIPLY

"Every child a wanted child," is the well-known slogan of the Planned Parenthood Foundation. It sounds wonderful, yet Planned Parenthood founder, Margaret Sanger, said, *"The most merciful thing a large family can do to one of its infant members is kill it."*[7]

In this motto dwells a deep-rooted lie that must be weeded out if we will ever restore a culture of life in America and reverse *Roe v. Wade.* What is that lie? It is that children who are not wanted can be discarded as mere products of conception by freedom of choice. God's solution to the scourge of abortion and the battle cry of the Church will be the same: "Every child a wanted child!"

This solution reflects a turning that must be seen in several areas:

- Hearts must be turned to wanting natural children.

- Hearts must be turned to adopting unwanted children, not only infants, but also older children and at-risk children.

- Hearts must be turned to spiritual parenting and mentoring youth into godly character and divine destiny.

- Hearts must be turned to the unsaved, with the Biblical emphasis of fathering converts into disciples of Jesus.

The "wanted child" issue actually strikes deeper than we care to look. The Church hasn't wanted children any more than the world has. The world has killed hers through abortion—the Church has closed her natural womb through contraception. That "wanting" must begin in the Church because it is the eternal Father's heart who said, "*I am seeking for a godly offspring*" (see Mal. 2:15). I am not against godly and wise family planning, but only in the context of aligning our hearts with God's Word and desires. We must deal with the "unwanted child" issue in ourselves before we condemn the world's "unwanted child" issues manifested in abortion. Please understand that I know there are many challenging physical and material circumstances that women and families face in regard to childbearing. God is full of grace. But are we really giving Him what He is seeking?

With deep sadness and inward frustration, I see the encroaching Muslim movement bearing offspring with about an 8 percent growth rate in America, rolling in over the once Christianized nations of the West. The population of the United States has a fertility rate of 2.1 percent. As it stands, our growth rate is barely enough to sustain itself.[8]

While the secular society is aborting their children, the Church imbibes the same humanistic lie that children are an inconvenience. We should obey the biblical culture plumb line that says, *"Children are a heritage of the lord...Happy is the man who has his quiver full of them"* (Ps. 127:4-5). Instead, we have adopted the lie that a large number of children born into a family were a blessing only for our past agrarian society. Rather than limiting our children to one or two per family, we could have shot four to ten God-given arrows into the heart of the voting booth. If we had, today there would be no pro-abortion leaders or judges in our government. We would have voted them out before there ever was a *Roe v. Wade.*

Let me speak clearly to my fellow reformation-minded brothers, sisters, and Christian leaders. If you believe that the Church is to exercise dominion in the earth, then I challenge you to repent and proclaim the unrescinded biblical mandate: Be fruitful, multiply, and subdue the earth with godly offspring (see Gen. 1:28). The Minister of Education in Poland shocked Europe with this statement:

> A nation that kills its children is a nation without a future. The continent that kills its children will be colonized by those who do not kill them....Abortion should be immediately prohibited....Human life is the highest value on earth.[9]

Someone told me he heard an interview of a Muslim woman in the Middle East saying essentially, "We will win this war. For I have 12 children and am still bearing at 50, while the women in America have two and quit bearing at 30." Recently I watched a documentary in which a Muslim leader declared that America will be an Islamic nation by the year 2050.[10] We need to obey the Bible! Sola Scriptura!

ADOPTION

The second area of turned hearts must be toward existing children—infants, orphans, and at-risk kids. To the pro-life argument that says that abortion may be killing future Martin Luther King Jr.s and Mother Theresas, pro-choice advocates may actually assert that it is more likely that we are killing future Charles Mansons or Joseph Stalins. I have actually read those kinds of arguments, but who is this that presumes to speak for God? Let the fathers and mothers of the Church respond, *"Give us your little Stalins and Mansons; we will father them and make them our Billy Grahams and Charles Colsons!"* The Church must not be just against abortion; it must become pro-life, pro-family, and pro-adoption. This is our revolution.

Just today I was speaking with Sammy Rodriguez, president of the National Association of Evangelicals for the Latinos in America. He said an adoption movement is taking place among the Latinos. In the last six months, families in one Latino Assembly of God Church have adopted 16 children. The movie *Bella,* staring Eduardo Verastegui, is a brilliant portrayal of the beauty of the pro-life Latino family and of adoption as the superior answer to abortion. Cindy Jacobs, noted author and prophet in the Body of Christ, prophesied three years ago that California would become a pro-life state. The only way that will happen is when the Latino people arise and vote for pro-life candidates and adopt babies by the thousands. Latino community, come save America!

TheCall is a national prayer ministry that gathers the Body of Christ together for massive solemn assemblies. It is based on Joel 2:15-16. *"Blow the trumpet in Zion, consecrate a fast, call a sacred assembly; gather the people...."* TheCall targets and mobilizes the young generation to fast and pray for righteousness and justice to be released in our nation. I rejoice in the many reports that we have received of adoptions that have been inspired through The Call solemn assemblies.

After TheCall Montgomery, it was reported that in one Church alone, 9 adoptions took place and 12 families became foster care certified.[11]

The Zoe Foundation, which came out of TheCall, exists to promote adoption as a positive alternative to abortion through educating the Church. It gathers lists of home study ready families and interested professionals, establishes birth mother care, and helps fund adoptions for families who understand prayer and fasting.[12] This foundation mobilizes adoption for babies that would have either been aborted in America or would have been thrown into the foster care system.

At the International House of Prayer (IHOP) in Kansas City, where we currently live, a remarkable adoption movement is taking place. What a thrill it is to see Down syndrome children from Romania, and potential child victims of the sexual trafficking industry being rescued and adopted. All of us know of the exorbitant costs of adoptions. The IHOP community has also established an adoption agency that will make adoptions more available by greatly reducing their costs. Something is wrong when adoptions are so expensive and abortions are relatively cheap. The Church must challenge this injustice.

It seems that everywhere across the world a great turning of hearts toward orphans and at-risk children is taking place. The spirit of Elijah is on the move (see Mal. 4:6). And it must be! Even this week a bill is being pushed forward in the House of Representatives that, if passed, will deny federal child welfare funds to states who hold laws that restrict homosexual, lesbian, and transgender adoptions.[13] If the Church doesn't move into this gap, the powers of darkness surely will. Maybe satan wants the children more than the Church does. God help us!

FATHER THE NEXT GENERATION

Lastly, we must turn our hearts to mentor the next generation, and we must turn our hearts to the lost—the sons and daughters who don't know the Father. A great harvest is coming, but where are the spiritual parents to disciple the new believers? It is not enough for sons to be born. Our goal must be to bring them to the place of character where they can shoulder government. *"Unto us a child is born, unto us a son is given; and the government shall be on His shoulder..."* (Isa. 9:6). Only mature sons and daughters who are discipled by godly men and women will be able to rule in the high places of cultural influence.

When fatherless leaders rule, fatherless rule follows and we have societal disintegration. As I gaze upon the landscape of the emerging generation, I find myself encouraged. They're not interested in a generation gap. They long for fathers. Let's give them what they yearn for. Forty years ago, a great Jesus movement erupted. Thousands of kids were saved, but where were the fathers? Kids three months old in the Lord were pastors. That promising harvest was lost in great measure. This time, God is preparing us to retain the harvest. Who will parent the newborns? Believe me, stadiums will be filled in this great awakening to come, but God will never bypass the process of fathering and discipleship.

A PRAYER THAT CHANGES THE WORLD

Recently, after an extended fast, I sensed the Lord speaking to me, "You will do more in your life by praying for your natural and spiritual sons and daughters than you will through your preaching." I have taken up a life assignment to regularly pray for between 15 and 20 double-portion sons and daughters.

James Dobson, the founder of Focus on the Family, relates that his father fasted and prayed for him every Saturday. James Dobson's life and ministry are truly an answer to prayer! Past Attorney General John Ashcroft tells of his father's prayers. In the mornings, little John would crawl under his father's legs as his dad kneeled and prayed something to the effect *"God, let my son go after noble pursuits."* And he grew up to become an attorney general—quite an answer from Heaven.[14]

I read in a *Guidepost* magazine of a Canadian university professor who reached out to a student from India named Bacht Singh. The young student went back to India. Fifty years later, a missionary couple visited the now-old professor. He asked them if, in all their years in India, they had ever heard of a man named Bacht Singh. They said, *"Why, Bacht Singh is one of the great church planters in India."* The professor responded, *"I have been praying for him every day for 50 years."* A week later the old man died. Oh, what a legacy of prayer![15]

Prayer will release a culture of life. Prayer will thrust men and women into the high places. Pray to the Lord of the Harvest to send forth laborers, to send forth sons and daughters into business, media, law, education, and politics. I'm praying for a young man that I believe will be the President of the United States some day. If you heard his prophetic history, you would know why I have such faith. Believe me, he's pro-life.

REDEFINING VOTING IN AMERICA

Whoever sheds man's blood, by man his blood shall be shed; for in the image of God He made man (Genesis 9:6).

The Genesis blueprint makes it clear that life is in the blood and that in the shedding of that innocent blood is the shattering of the image of God. As I write about this great moral tragedy of abortion, let me ask the question, *"Is there any difference between the blood of the preborn baby and the newly born baby?"* No, a thousand times no!

Today innocent blood is being shed through the legal decree of abortion. The psalmist in Psalm 94:20-21 declared:

Shall the throne of iniquity, which devises evil by law [government that legalizes evil] have fellowship with You [God]? They gather together against the life of the righteous, and condemn innocent blood (Psalm 94:20-21).

God will not have fellowship with a government that practices iniquity by passing laws legalizing the shedding of innocent blood through abortion. Our American leaders will be held accountable for this blatant rebellion against the Lord and the very foundational law of God, *"You shall not murder"* (Exod. 20:13).

However, in America, it is not the president and the Congress who are the ultimate leaders. We are a government of the people, by the people, and for the people. Our government officials are elected by us! Therefore, when we vote for those who rule for abortion and against the sanctity of marriage, God will actually hold us accountable for throwing off His fetters of law (see Ps. 2). If we vote for ungodly leaders, we actually are having fellowship with a throne of iniquity and we have joined the conspiracy of governmental leaders who are warned in Psalm 2.

Therefore, be wise, O kings; be instructed you judges of the earth (Ps. 2:10). Put your name where *kings* and *judges* are in that Scripture because in a democracy you are the kings and as such must answer to the Lord's warning. *"Therefore, be wise, Lou; be instructed, Lou."*

We are redefining voting for the Christian. Voting is not a light political choice that you make because you have a warm feeling about someone's charisma or their promise to change the economy. Instead, it is an act of conscience and a prophetic witness to a higher King and a higher law. The constitution of the "Kingdom Hill" that confronts the rebellion of Capitol Hill is the Ten Commandments, and in our present case of abortion, it commands the higher loyalty of its Kingdom constituents with the unalterable word of authority, *"You shall not murder"* (Exod. 20:13).

William Wilberforce challenged the politics of neutrality and the moral vacillation of his society. He declared concerning the murderous slave trade of his time:

> There is a principle above everything that is political, and when I reflect on the command that says, "thou shall do no murder" believing the authority to be divine [Sola Scriptura], how can I dare to set out any reasoning of my own against it. And when we think of eternity and of the future consequences of all human conduct what is there in this life that could make any man contradict the dictates of his conscience, the principles of justice, the laws of religion, and of God.[16]

Wilberforce actually believed that he would be held eternally accountable if he supported the slave trade. He considered his vote as an act of murder. Brothers and sisters, we ought to tremble at the voting booth and teach our children to tremble. In a democracy, a culture of life will only be upheld if the righteous will vote in mass for candidates who stand for life. No prayer and no social action can take that place. *Vote life!*

SHAPING HISTORY THROUGH FASTING AND PRAYER

In 1996, during a 40-day fast, I had a dream in which I saw a Buddhist House of Prayer sitting on top of a Christian House of Prayer and dominating it. Suddenly, the Christian House of Prayer did a reversal and began to dominate the Buddhist House of Prayer. Through this dream, God gave me my life job description. *"Raise up a House of Prayer that contends with every other house that exalts itself above the supremacy and authority of Christ."*

Behind the promotion of the world's strong leaders and their false ideologies are unseen demonic powers that are seeking to shape a culture hostile to the Kingdom of God. If we are going to shift a nation to a culture of life, we must once again reclaim the power of Heaven-affecting prayer, which can alone deal with the source of societal breakdown in the earth—the principalities and powers. Consider the testimony of Daniel's fast.

> *Do not fear, Daniel, for from the first day that you set your heart to understand, and to humble yourself before your God, your words were heard; and I have come because of your words. But the prince of the kingdom of Persia withstood me twenty-one days; and behold, Michael, one of the chief princes, came to help me, for I had been left alone there with the kings of Persia* (Daniel 10:12-13).

Daniel 10 describes a supernatural conflict between heavenly archangels and the demonic angel, the prince of Persia. This dark spiritual prince of Persia was playing the puppet strings over the earthly king of Persia as a part of satan's plan to hinder the people of God. Daniel initiated a sustained fast that inaugurated war in the heavens. The battle ensued for 21 days until the heavenly angel broke through to give understanding to Daniel.

> That Daniel's visitor is said to have "remained there with the kings of Persia" is best taken to mean that he remained preeminent (as on a field of battle, standing victorious), having won this struggle, and therefore he had the desired influence over the kings of Persia....This

suggests that the conflict waged had been basically over this position of influence. Satan's emissary had held it, thus working to the detriment of God's program and people: But God's angel had come and fought him for it, no doubt as a part of his assigned mission in coming to Daniel, and had defeated him.[17]

The implications of this passage are earthshaking. When kings and rulers are passing antichrist legislation or when universities are dominated by the teaching of false philosophies, you know that there are spiritual powers influencing them. But when praying people set themselves to fast, amazing shifts can occur because the angelic realm has dislodged the demonic and gained the place of influence.

Once again, consider the affect of fasting and prayer in the book of Esther. Queen Esther fasted three days, appealing to the Supreme Court of Heaven to overrule the Supreme Court of Haman and his death decree against the Jews. Within three days, Haman was hung, Mordecai was promoted, and the whole Persian public policy toward the Jews was shifted. If you could have pulled back the heavenly curtains, you would have seen principalities and powers dislodged and angels gaining the place of influence over the Persian government. The result of that heavenly battle was manifested in the raising up and pulling down of kings.

Could this be the reason that the ungodly hold the places of influence in the seven mountains of culture today? Could it be because the Church has lost air supremacy in the heavens?

It has confined its interest to earth and ignored its responsibility in the heavens. Should we not encourage each other to gain imperial perspective in our praying?[18]

Until we win this spiritual battle, there will be no reformation.

Five years ago, at TheCall School, we received a dream in which I was a referee on a basketball court, and young people were there weeping because of the presence of a demonic barrier on that court. In the dream a 17-year-old woman cried out, *"Lou Engle, it's your turn now!"* I took the hands of those kids and swept that barrier off the court.

The definition of *referee* is a judge over the court. We sensed God was calling us to gain a place of spiritual authority in prayer over the powers affecting the Supreme Court. Three days before the elections in 2004, we needed a pro-life president who would appoint pro-life judges. Seventy kids standing in front of the Supreme Court did an Esther fast—no food or water for three days. At that time, I was invited to take a tour of the Supreme Court. When I asked the young lady taking me on the tour if there was a basketball court in the Supreme Court building, she said, *"As a matter of fact there is, and it is exactly on top of where the Supreme Court holds its hearings. They call it 'The highest Court in the land.'"*

I said, "Take me to that court!" Standing on that basketball court, with the U.S. Supreme court beneath the feet of Jesus and my feet, I declared, "From this day forward there will only be pro-life judges."

After the elections, we launched a House of Prayer with up to 70 young people praying day and night facing the Supreme Court building. A week before President George W. Bush was to appoint a Justice to replace William Rehnquist, one of our young women, knowing nothing, dreamed that a man named John Roberts would become the next Supreme Court Justice. Those kids prayed. Don't you think they were baptized in confidence before God when the president nominated John Roberts for the position of Supreme Court Chief Justice?

We believe that through intensive, focused, day-and-night prayer and fasting, principalities and powers were shifted, and God got His pro-life man to the top of the Supreme Court Mountain. Those kids had one job description—through prayer and fasting, to rule over the principalities and powers influencing the Supreme Court to legalize abortion. In similar fashion, years ago my friend, Tom Hess, fasted and prayed in a condo facing the Supreme Court building for a pro-life judge. On the 39th day a pro-abortion judge, Justice John Marshall Harlan, resigned and a pro-life judge, Justice William Rehnquist, took his place.

There is a new breed of praying, passionate young men and women on the horizon; they have been fasting and praying for justice. They may become the *"ecclesia"* that Jesus spoke about, that the gates of hell or the "powers of death" would not prevail against (see Matt. 16:18).

A young Korean, who is a spiritual son of mine, maintained a Daniel fast, praying for the ending of abortion and for a pro-life president. For two years, he ate no meat or sweets. The day after pro-life President George W. Bush was reelected in 2004, the young man said to the Lord, *"Unless you confirm to me today that you want me to continue on my Daniel fast, I am going to break it at midnight and eat cake."* That evening as he walked to his school library to study, he met a young man. He introduced himself saying, *"Hello, my name is Brian Kim."*

The student replied, "Hello, my name is Daniel Fast." People are shocked when they hear the story, and they laugh, but it's no laughing matter. God was saying, "Young man, you are highly esteemed in Heaven. You are moving angels and demons. Go on fasting until this murderous slave trade is expelled from the nation."

This young man dreamed of a strategy of prayer to target abortion. Fasting opens up revelation. In the dream, people had tape over their mouths with the word LIFE written on it. For five years now, in response to that dream, through a ministry called Bound4LIFE, people have stood with LIFE tape over their mouths, pleading the blood of Jesus over the bloodshed of

America, crying for mercy and justice. Who would have guessed that the media would fall in love with the image and blast it out on television news programs, national newspapers, and magazines all over the world?

Now, across America, thousands have prayed in front of courts and abortion clinics with LIFE tape, pleading a 22-word prayer, "Jesus, I plead your blood over my sins and the sins of my nation. God, end abortion and send revival to America." Bound4LIFE chapters are spreading across the land. Amazingly, April 26, 2008, 6,200 intercessors stood before their state supreme courts, pled the blood of Jesus, and cried for abortion to end. Beginning that day, and for five months afterward, in rain and heat, young intercessors stood in front of the Supreme Court contending for LIFE. We were stunned recently while looking at four polls that described a sudden jump in pro-life opinion in America and a massive fall in pro-choice opinion whose beginning coincided with the five months of prayer.[19]

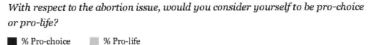

With respect to the abortion issue, would you consider yourself to be pro-choice or pro-life?

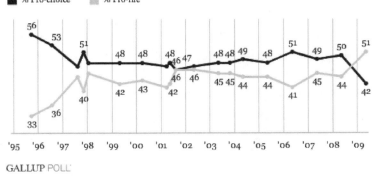

GALLUP POLL

Could this shift in public opinion reflect that demonic powers were being evicted from the social conscience of a nation? If so, then the ideology of homosexual marriage can also be challenged by the praying Church. The pornography hell holes in Northridge, California, can be shaken. Hollywood can become Holywood as God raises up voices in response to the prayers of His people. Where there is prevailing prayer, there is no safe place for the devil. For too long the Church has toyed around with prayer. God is looking for a Contending House of Prayer.

CHANGING BEHAVIOR THROUGH FASTING AND PRAYER

Fasting and prayer can shift the powers over governments. They can also shift the minds of individuals who are considering having an abortion. In 1992, a young woman walked into an abortion clinic with her boyfriend. They filled out the paper work, paid for the abortion, did her blood work, and had a sonogram to determine the exact stage of her pregnancy. The young woman waited anxiously for her name to be called, but heard, *"Not this one!"* She turned to her boyfriend, "What did you say?"

"Nothing," he responded.

"You said something," she argued. Nervous, she looked around the room, amazed at the number of girls waiting for abortions. Once again she heard a voice, *"Look how many will die today; **not…this… one!**"* Angry she turned to her boyfriend, "What did you say?"

"Nothing," he defended.

A nurse called her name with about 25 other girls. *"First, does anyone have a doubt in their mind?"* The nurse asked. Without a second thought, the young woman's hand shot up. The nurse looked her straight in the eyes and said, "We will still be here in a week, and you'll still be pregnant. Go figure it out."

The young woman believes this nurse was an angel on assignment. The young woman walked out to the waiting room and tapped her boyfriend on the shoulder. "What are you doing?" he asked.

"Looks like we're having a baby?" She replied.

He jumped up and yelled, "We're having a baby!" Her boyfriend ran up to the front desk and slapped his hand on the counter. "Give us our money back. We have to buy a crib. We're having a baby!"

Sixteen years later, that child was a godly young man in my daughter's school, the Daniel Academy. God is pro-life, and I have the feeling that he is shouting *"No, not this one!"* for every unborn child and every mother that is thinking about having an abortion.

At TheCall, we are burning with a prayer vision called *"No, Not This One."* Here in Kansas City, a Crisis Pregnancy counselor sends us SOS text prayer alerts (not using names or private information), when a woman still wants to have an abortion after her counseling. Immediately, 30 to 40 people are texted, and everyone is praying a crisis prayer. We take a stand against the powers of death and pray for the life of the unborn child. We don't just pray for the life, but we dedicate that child and all the days of his or her life to the Lord in prayer. We also pray for the mother and father to find God's wisdom, guidance, and provision in their moment of crisis. Here are some of our SOS text miracles:

- SOS TEXT: Woman still set on abortion after seeing ultrasound yesterday. She is extremely detached from her pregnancy.

- **ANSWER TO PRAYER TEXT:** She decided to keep the baby!! God did a miracle! She said, *"I just started to think more about it."*

- SOS TEXT: 1st trimester woman pressured to abort. Pray her / his heart turn towards child.

- **ANSWER TO PRAYER TEXT:** The woman who was being pressured to abort by boyfriend said he has decided that they should keep the baby!!! She said it was truly an act of God and answer to prayer.

In this battle for life, I believe every Church needs to adopt a Crisis Pregnancy Center. This is where the rubber meets the road. May there be *"No, not this one"* intercessors for every Crisis Pregnancy Center in America. We need to finance and serve these Crisis Pregnancy Centers. Most of them are severely strapped for funds. Why should Planned Parenthood have all the money? Have you known the God who cries out with anger, *"I beat My fists at the dishonest profit which you have made, and at the bloodshed which has been in your midst"* (Ezek. 22:13). God beats His fists when He sees the profit of Planned Parenthood through the shedding of the blood of babies.

I wonder how He feels when Crisis Pregnancy Centers and pro-life movements live on a shoestring. Maybe He beats His fists at the Church for its lack of concern and its unwillingness to finance this new Underground Railroad. Thank God for Focus on the Family, a Christian nonprofit organization committed to the institution of family according to biblical truth; they funded the purchase of hundreds of ultrasound machines for Crisis Pregnancy Centers.[20] When women see an ultrasound, over 79 percent keep their babies.[21]

In the days of slavery, the wealthy Tappan brothers vowed to live only on what they needed and devote the rest of their finances to abolition and revival.[22] In this new defining issue of justice in our day, we need the Tappans again. The Church must be committed to provide housing, care, and mentoring programs for pregnant mothers facing agonizing circumstances when they decide to keep their babies.

EVERY VOICE MUST BE COUNTED

When Jesus saw the multitudes that were harassed and helpless like sheep without a shepherd, He turned and spoke to his disciples, commanding them, *"Therefore pray the Lord of the harvest to send out laborers into His harvest"* (Matt. 9:38). God wants to thrust forth laborers, brilliant men and women, into the high places of ideological influence where they can shape the future of our cities and nations. If we are going to have a culture of life, believers have to be in the middle of the PTA, the law schools, and the education system. Fearless prophets need to be in the pulpits.

Just think, Hollywood preaches to more people in one night than most preachers preach to in their whole lifetime. We need pro-life screenwriters. God give us pro-life voices to challenge the prophets of Baal in the high places of news and media. Give us musicians with influence like Bono who will sing songs about the ending of abortion, not just politically correct songs inspiring people to feed the poor. I believe Bono would be vilified if he took on the pro-life issue. The places where there is the most pressure to be politically correct are the places where demons are actually raging the most. Jezebel will always seek to silence the prophets. We need a young generation of people who will turn their talents into tremors that shake injustice.

For every revolution, someone needs to preach it, praise it, print it, pray it, paint it, and promote it. In every arena of judicial crisis for justice, God always has an Esther being prepared in the background. Where there's a Hitler, God has a Churchill. Where there's a Jezebel, there is an Elijah being prepared. The only question that remains is, will the people who have been prepared seize their moments and risk everything, renouncing self-preservation to become the hinge of history.

In the days of slavery, a young Harriet Beecher Stowe was challenged by her sister-in-law:

"Hattie, if I could use a pen as you can, I would write something which would make this whole nation feel what an accursed thing slavery is." Hattie rose up from her chair, crushed the letter in her hand, and with an expression in her face that stamped itself on the mind of her son vowed, "I will write something! I will if I live."[23]

She wrote the book, *Uncle Tom's Cabin*. By the end of the first year of printing, 300,000 copies had been sold, which was an unheard of publishing phenomenon in her day. When Abraham Lincoln met with her, he greeted Hattie as *the little lady who started the Great War.*[24] God give us writers who can shake this altar of death and subpoena the conscience of the nation through books that come from Heaven.

The young people in D.C. were given a dream that the key to ending abortion would be found in a series of old books. The following day a man sent us an email and said he believes there is an old book that holds the key for the ending of abortion, *Horton Hears a Who* by Dr. Seuss.[25] The theme of the book is *"A person's a person no matter how small and every voice must be counted."* We began to pray that God would raise up voices—in arts, in media, in every sphere, who would speak out against abortion and bring a culture of life. What encouragement swept into our hearts when Fox Movies put out *"Horton Hears A Who."* God is shouting to the nation, *"Every voice must be counted if abortion is going to end!"*

That same year, movies exalting adoption over the decision of abortion were released, including *Bella* and *Juno*. On a regular basis I pray the Jabez prayer, *"Oh that you would bless me indeed, and extend Your influence through me! God lay Your hand upon me! Supernaturally endorse my life and deliver me from satan's schemes!"* (my paraphrase of 1 Chron. 4:10). It's not enough to believe that God is great; we need a generation of those who believe and pray, *"God, live great through me! Make my life extraordinary! Give me a voice!"*

Every voice must be counted. Movements like Operation Outcry and Silent No More are mobilizing the voice of an army of women who have had abortions and who are crying out boldly, *"Abortion was not good for me, and it is not good for women."* I pray for that precious woman, wherever she is, who cried, *"I'm a murderer, I'm a murderer!"* God turn her pain into a prayer that produces a prophecy that changes a nation. "Abortion is not something that happens and you just go on with your life. You go on as a very wounded individual. I don't want other women to experience the pain that I have had," said Rebecca Porter, Florida state leader for Operation Outcry.[26]

According to Matthew Lockett, director of Bound4LIFE, over 350,000 people in America have put on the life bands that are available through Bound4LIFE.[27]

My dream is that a million Americans will take this life band and make a covenant saying: "Every time I look at this band, I will pray for the ending of abortion. Jesus, I plead your blood over my sins and the sins of my nation. God end abortion and send revival to America." Next, they will covenant saying "I will never vote for anyone who is pro-choice." And then they will covenant saying, "I will obey God as He leads me into acts of justice and mercy to touch the world under the sentence of death with the broken, bleeding, loving heart of Jesus." Let every voice be counted. If we find our voice, America could turn back to a culture of life.

Chapter 6

REFORMATION OF MARRIAGE

JIM GARLOW

Pledge 6: I will focus on strengthening
and prioritizing my own family and will
not allow the sacred covenant of marriage
between a man and a woman to be
constitutionally redefined (see Gen. 2:24).

Marriage is under assault, severe assault. It is not by accident that the evil one has focused on this particular institution. Although satan is not all knowing—omniscience belongs exclusively to God—the devil does have sufficient awareness to know that destroying the more than 5,000-year-old institution of one man-one woman marriage is critical to his world domination.

It is for this reason that pro-gay marriage leader and radical, San Francisco Mayor Gavin Newsom, who performed the first illegal homosexual "weddings," which precipitated a massive statewide defense of marriage in California, said on August 5, 2008, "If we lose, our movement will be dealt a blow that will set us back on a whole range of issues."[1]

He understood then, and understands now, what is at stake. People who are against biblical, traditional, natural marriage "get it." They know what is at stake. My question to you is: "Do you, as a follower of Christ, 'get it?' That is, do you understand what is at stake in the global and cosmic defense of marriage?"

Allow me to cut to the chase. God established marriage. Period. In the first few pages of Genesis, God established three things—in this order:

- Male and female, that is, gender specificity

- Marriage of one man and one woman

- Birth

Attempting to decimate what God had established, the evil one has introduced, in reverse order as above, the following:

- Abortion, resulting in the murder of millions of preborn babies, thus mitigating against the miracle of birth established by God

- The redefinition of marriage, the rejection of God's definition

- The loss of gender specificity, through transgenderism, transexuality, bisexuality, and cross-dressing, thereby mitigating against God's creation of male and female

It is not by accident that the evil one intends to undo that which God established.

A STORY

To make the case for marriage, allow me to share a story. It is the story of one state, California. You might be tempted to say, "Well I don't live in California, so I will skip this chapter." Resist that temptation.

Although my story is set in that state, the story is really about us all. As I walk with you down a historical pathway covering two and a half years, from mid-2007 to the end of 2009, don't miss the *real* story. The issue is really *not* what happened in California. Nor is it about that particular two-year span. It is about principles, principles that apply to you now. They are timeless principles. So don't become bogged down in the details of the California story. Instead, allow the key eternal truths about society's most endangered institution to grip you. In this historical account are many timeless principles and truths. Watch for them. Commit them to your heart.

This story is mine, as well as many other Californians, but its axioms regarding marriage need to be yours! Read carefully!

THE MAYOR WHO SPARKED A MOVEMENT

"What are you going to do about it?" the caller asked. In his exuberance, I am not even sure if he identified himself before posing the question. It was September 2007. Jimmy Valentine, producer of the popular Roger Hedgecock Radio Show—on KOGO radio in San Diego, since syndicated nationwide—called me and asked with great intensity, "What are you going to do about it?"

"About what?" I asked.

He continued, "About our mayor's flip-flop on marriage, now coming out in favor of so-called same sex marriage?"

Valentine, following Hedgecock's lead, suggested to me the possibility of a massive protest rally to be held somewhere like Qualcomm Stadium, home of the San Diego Chargers. Although calls for such a rally seemed at that moment to be premature, that phone call was the "seed" that energized Christian activists in San Diego.

Ingredient 1: A Movement

A few days later, as I sat with eight like-minded and highly passionate people around a table in a Sunday school room of a small Baptist Church in San Diego, a God-given strategy was born. It became a portion of the strategy that would help to secure the needed signatures to qualify an amendment, Proposition 8, for the ballot and to eventually see it pass. A tight and committed group emerged that night to help evangelical pastors and churches in California unify and rise to the challenge.

Several days later, in October 2007, nearly 200 pastors and Christian leaders gathered; meetings in December 2007 and January 2008 followed. A movement was born.

Ingredient 2: Foundational Truths

To keep us all "on the same page" and to prevent the new movement from derailing, the attendees unofficially, by applause as it was read, embraced "The 10 Declarations for Protecting Biblical Marriage: Principles to Unite, Focus and Ground Us During This Precarious Season." The document served as a guide to how the campaign would be operated. I wrote it the night before our first meeting in an attempt to stay "on the road" and avoid two "ditches:" gay bashing in one ditch and cowardice in the other.

We affirmed that:

1. God loves all people; therefore, we love all people, and we will do so regardless of how some view or define themselves sexually. We choose to love those who, for whatever reason, have chosen to involve themselves in homosexual or other unbiblical sexual activity.

2. The Bible defines marriage as a covenantal union of one male and one female, which provides the foundation for healthy, whole family life.

3. While the Bible may not address sexual orientation, it does, however, clearly address sexual actions. We will not expend endless energy debating what people claim they "are" (homosexual). We focus instead on what persons choose to "do" (homosexual acts).

4. We choose to be Christ-like even when we are falsely accused and slandered. *"A gentle answer turns away wrath, but a harsh word stirs up anger"* (Prov. 15:1). With Christ's patient help, we shall attempt to evidence "a gentle answer" to all.

5. As the Church, we repent of our nation's moral condition. The reason for our present dilemma is not that there are assertive and demanding homosexuals or biblically ignorant judges or even a scripturally devoid electorate. It is easy to focus on these as the cause of the problem. But the real dilemma is ultimately a

spiritually impotent Church, which through failure to adequately teach and model authentic Christianity, has allowed and caused ungodly people to be elected, who in turn selected unbiblical judges.

6. We cry out for spiritual renewal in our state, nation, and world. Winning a vote to defend traditional marriage is of prime importance in the short term. But long-term spiritual renewal, revival, and evangelism are ultimately the real answer to this situation.

7. We refuse the false choice between temporal and spiritual means, since both are used to advance Christ's Kingdom. While we will diligently urge people who understand truth to register and vote, we give ourselves to the Word, sacraments, prayer, fasting, intercession, personal holy living, and the standard Christian disciplines.

8. We repent of our failure to adequately and effectively protect biblical, heterosexual marriage. The divorce rate is an abomination to God, a curse on the world and nation, and an anathema to us. We repent of our failure to adequately sanctify marriages in a way that would cause them to endure the pressures of daily temptations and duress.

9. Being approved by people is not to be valued over the conformity to God's will, ways, and Word.

We will not be people-pleasers. We choose to be bold, yet loving; firm, yet compassionate. We will not be intimidated by the attacks of those who oppose biblical marriage. We understand that political correctness and biblical integrity are incompatible.

10. By God's strength and grace, we will be faithful...to the end. We will never abandon His Word. We will never capitulate or compromise. If we are harassed, jailed, imprisoned, driven underground, or even killed, we will be found worthy of joining the saints and martyrs who have gone before us. Whether here or in the world to come, due to our unswerving dedication to our heavenly Father, His Word, and our King and Savior Jesus, we shall overcome.

Ingredient 3: Prayer

We knew and understood that our greatest work could not ultimately "save" marriage in our state. Sensing that prayer would be crucial, we asked dynamic prayer leader, Lou Engle of TheCall, to uproot his wife and seven children and move from Kansas City to San Diego for six months for the purpose of putting together a prayer foundation for the campaign.

The prayer goal became twofold:

1. In the short term, to see Proposition 8 passed at the November 2008 election

2. To see a spiritual awakening happen in the hearts of Californians

Ingredient 4: Unity

In addition to agreed upon principles (The Ten Declarations of Marriage) and a solid prayer base (40 days of fasting and praying), we knew that we could not succeed without unity. By the time of the second meeting in late 2007, there was great unity among participating Bible-believing pastors in San Diego. Egos and logos, along with denominational differences, were laid aside. We all worked in such a way that no one could get the credit. And to this day, long after the victory, we all know that *no one person* can take credit for this victory. It took *all* of us!

Ingredient 5: Short-Term Strategy

But we needed more: we needed a God-given, Holy Spirit breathed strategy. It soon came. The pastoral team developed a strategy to collect the necessary signatures, 694,000 to be exact, to get a marriage initiative on the November ballot that, if passed, would be put into the state constitution. We knew that we would need to gather more than 1.1 million signatures in order to ensure that we had enough to make up for any signatures not considered valid.

San Diego pastors, along with some God fearing attorneys, began "exporting" the "San Diego model" of organizing pastors into both Los Angeles and Orange Counties in order to facilitate collecting of the necessary signatures. The San Diego pastors connected with concerned and active pastors in those counties, asking them to gather other pastors and meet with the San Diego team in meetings in February 2008.

These "sparks of Orange County and the LA area," already lit by alert pastors, merged with the efforts of the San Diego team. In addition, some 40 different para-Church organizations were merging their efforts under the Website ProtectMarriage.com, providing an umbrella of superb overall leadership to the entire state. Key ministries began to respond to the "Macedonian calls" from California, asking for outside help for the Herculean task. They responded with generosity, from Washington, D.C., and other locations, bringing with them years of experience, resources, and political savvy.

As the "pastors-in-defense-of-marriage" movement spread, they discovered and combined forces with pastors in other places who were also stirred to action, in some cases already having significant momentum. Thanks to the power of the Holy Spirit, we became much more than the sum total of our individual parts.

Ingredient 6: Authentic Ecumenicity

While the evangelical pastors organized to generate volunteers, Catholic leaders came together to provide the finances to hire professional signature gatherers. Most significant was the role of the National Organization for Marriage, a Princeton, New Jersey, based Catholic marriage organization skilled in both fund-raising and media presence.

Visible Catholic businesspersons proved to be essential to the campaign's success. Hostile, anti-marriage forces later targeted them in an attempt to intimidate and punish. A courageous San Diego Roman Catholic bishop, who later moved to Oakland, California, proved to be one of the pillars of the campaign, becoming a hero to all the evangelicals. He played a key role, both in our county and in the state, in the passage of Prop 8. As a result, the California Pastors Rapid Response Team and their laity produced nearly 45 percent of the signatures, and the professional signature gatherers hired by the Catholic group produced over 55 percent. Together we did it!

What accounted for the effectiveness of this merged effort? The answer is in what I refer to as "the grand re-alignment." Allow me to explain. I love Church history. To many people, the thought of reading a Church history book is a real "yawner," a profoundly effective sedative. Not to me. I promise not to bore you, if you will bear with me for a significant explanation of what God has done in recent years.

From the early 1500s until the past century, Catholics and Protestants had little trust for each other. The "grand divide" was obvious. It was Catholics vs. Protestants. However, that changed when liberalism made its debut in the late 1800s and early 1900s, having full impact by the mid-1900s. Liberalism, at its core, is disbelief in the authenticity and authority of the Bible.

During the 1960s and following, Protestants were divided into "liberals," those who no longer accepted the Scriptures as God's Word, and "conservatives," those who adhered to the Scriptures. At the same time, Catholics went through their own "liberal/conservative" split. The result? The fissure now falls in different places. As a conservative, Bible-believing, Protestant evangelical, I have more in common with a conservative Catholic than I do with a liberal Protestant. Conservative evangelicals and conservative Catholics share the same reverence for such time-honored doctrines as the virgin birth, the deity of Christ, the atonement in the crucifixion, and the reality of the resurrection.

With Scripture as our common bond, conservative Catholics and evangelicals found themselves very comfortable sharing the same "foxholes" in the Prop 8 battle, with our "weapons" pointed in the same direction. In contrast to liberal Catholics and liberal Protestants, who find oneness based on that which they no longer believe, we found ourselves working joyously with Catholics based on our common honoring of the Scriptures' teaching on the sanctity of marriage.

Ingredient 7: Bridging

One of the lessons we needed to learn was how to "bridge" to groups well outside our comfort zone: Hindus, Sikhs, and Muslims, as examples. But the one group that proved to be most significant in the Prop 8 victory was Mormons. They approached us before we were inclined to approach them. In the first meeting they discussed the obvious "elephant in the room." "We will *not*," they emphatically stated, "attempt to proselytize your people." And they honored their word throughout the entire campaign.

What we did not anticipate was that Mormons were most suited for what was ahead in the campaign, specifically the door-to-door canvassing, as that is built into their spiritual DNA. Also, they could handle the rejection often associated with the campaign. Lastly, they had the logistics in place that made it possible for us to divide the state up quickly and begin canvassing. And when we finally went out knocking on doors, they were 24,000 of the 25,000 who showed up the first weekend.

Most importantly, they are organized as a hierarchical entity; thus one letter from a high-ranking LDS (Church of Jesus Christ of Latter Day Saints, or Mormons) official triggers an immediate response. The result was that the Mormons provided not only the lion's share of workers, even though only 2 percent of the state's population, they also funded over 40 percent of the cost of the entire campaign.

Not sure quite how to relate to each other, I stated one day, "We are not theological brothers and sisters, but we are friends and neighbors." And that became a satisfactory foundation for a wonderful working relationship. I had the privilege of going to Salt Lake City and meeting with some of the top echelon of the LDS church and thanking them for their amazing sacrifice and work.

One of them stated aphoristically, "We have to learn how to somehow put up with each other's theology, and we will, as we work together." And that proved to be the case. The important lesson: God taught us to "bridge" for His Glory. And we did. When the Mormons were viciously attacked after the Prop 8 victory, Catholics and Evangelicals flocked to defend them because they had become "our friends and our neighbors."

Ingredient 8: A Long-Term Strategy

As noted at the outset, our story to bring about the "reformation of marriage" is showcased in one state's battle to defend it. A timeline might prove helpful to grasp the intensity of the struggle:

- April 2007: Our movement reached the goal of 1.1 million signatures, officially qualifying the measure to be voted on as an *amendment to the state constitution* as a November ballot initiative by the end of April. This did not occur a moment too early.

- May 2007: A few days later, supporters of traditional, natural marriage discovered how badly the ballot initiative would be needed. As forecasted, in May 2007, the California Supreme Court overturned Proposition 22 (affirming one man-one woman marriage) from the California Family Code (as opposed to the state constitution).

- June 2007: Therefore, so-called same-sex "marriage" was legal in California as of June 16, 2008, at 5:00 P.M. The push to add an amendment to the state constitution became even more necessary.

In the face of these events, our long-term strategy formed: communication, activation, and prayer. But how should we verbalize the need to protect marriage to the many unchurched people who would need to be convinced? To assist in this task, state marriage leaders began a laborious process of messaging, focus groups, and polling. Through this process, the message tightened in its clarity and focus.

PART I:
COMMUNICATION

But there were challenges. California is a very large state, with nearly 40 million residents. How could we reach pastors scattered across an entire state? At this point, some activated pastors developed the idea to not merely meet together in one place, but to have people meet at various locations around the state and be linked together via conference calls and later via webinars. By the second statewide webinar / call in July 2008, 3,000 pastors and Christian leaders gathered together in 175 locations in California, along with 300 pastors in Florida, and 100 pastors in Arizona, two states also facing a vote on marriage.

PROTECT MARRIAGE
CALIFORNIA TIMELINE
JUNE 25 - NOV 6, 2008

	August	September	October
"Parish" Walking:	Voter ID (Registered)	Advocacy (Undecided/Pro)	Get Out The Vote (Pro)
Phoning:		Internal Church Phoning	

iProtect Youth Rally Oct 1

Family Voting Weekend pray and vote together as a family Sat & Sun Oct 18 – 19

Absentee Ballot Request Deadline Oct 28

Deadline for Absentee Ballots to be turned in to Registrar's office Nov 4

"Blow the Trumpet" Day — Joel 2

Preach on Fasting - Receive Offering for Protect Marriage Sunday Sept 21

End 100 Days of Prayer

Preach on Prayer Sunday July 27

Begin 100 Days of Prayer July 28

Voter Regist. Sunday Aug 3

TheCall Video and Postcards Sunday Sept 7

Begin 40 Day Fast Wednesday Sept 24

Begin Absentee Voting Oct 6

Preach on Marriage Month of October

Voter Registration Deadline Oct 20

TheCall Qualcomm Stadium 10 am – 10 pm Saturday Nov 1

End 40 Day Fast Sunday Nov 2

Election Day Nov 4 (Take Vacation Day?)

Pastors Conference Call	Pastors Conference Call	Pastors Conference Call	Pastors Conference Call	Pastors Conference Call	Pastors Conference Call	Pastors Conference Call
Wednesday June 25 10 am 101 Locations 1600+ Pastors	Wednesday July 30 10 am Goal: 200 Locations 2000 Pastors	Wednesday Aug 27 10 am Goal: 200 Locations 2500 Pastors	Wednesday Sept 24 10 am Goal: 300 Locations 4500 Pastors	Wednesday Oct 8 10 am Goal: 350 Locations 5250 Pastors	Wednesday Oct 22 10 am Goal: 400 Locations 6000 Pastors	Thursday Nov 6 10 am

The seven webinars, three satellite simulcasts, knocking on doors campaigns, and telephone campaigns followed this schedule:

- Having certain pastors articulate the complete biblical underpinnings of scriptural marriage. This could be accomplished through our webinars.

- Encouraging pastors to establish scriptural understandings in their congregations. This could be accomplished by equipping pastors in our webinars.

- Helping laypeople grasp the severe political consequences when the state has a vested interest in affirming same sex "marriage." For this we needed to do costly satellite seminars.

- Assisting churched people in articulating a case for traditional marriage without using any Bible verses, but using only social science. For this we needed access to congregations, via video events, and during evening hours when laypeople were not at work.

THE BIBLICAL BASIS OF MARRIAGE

To make certain that all pastors were grasping the weight and force of the scriptural understanding of marriage, we shared "The Biblical Foundations of the Marriage Debate."

Why do you support marriage? The answer may not be as obvious as you might think. There are three prongs to this:

- The Genesis "image of God" teaching

- Jesus' own words on marriage

- The book of Revelation's "Marriage of the Lamb" account

Simply stated, the Bible begins with a marriage and ends with a wedding. Why? The answer is what propelled many to risk so much to stand for marriage in California. What follows is the "core" of this entire chapter. We shall never have authentic "reformation of marriage" unless we understand the Genesis-Revelation connection.

GENESIS: THE *FULL* IMAGE OF GOD

We know that God is neither male nor female. Yet we are made "in His image" (see Gen. 1:27). In spite of the fact that we are, as individuals, made in the image of God, the true, full image is expressed when the two halves of humanity complement each other and become one.

If I understand the role of marriage properly, a male, by himself, is not fully representative of all the descriptors of the image of God. For example, a male, by himself, cannot manifest the full spectrum of God's features, historically associated with both femininity (tenderness) and masculinity (strength). Thus, no husband, for example, can fully represent the image of God.

At the same time, if I understand the early pages of Genesis correctly, a female, by herself, cannot do justice to the full spectrum of the image of God.

However, when the two complementary halves of humanity unite—physically, spiritually, mentally, emotionally, and psychologically—the image of God, containing both tenderness and strength, is manifested. Male and female are made anatomically, emotionally, and spiritually for oneness. Husband and wife, joined together, represent the full spectrum of the image of God.

One part of God's image is His creativity. In sexual union, husband and wife become co-creators, in a sense, with God, in their act of procreation. Children come into being as husband and wife unite, and each child is one more expression of the image (creativity) of God. A sperm and an egg unite to form (miraculously) a human! A person! Male and female becoming one is what Genesis establishes as the components for this image. The breathtaking image of God! Creating! No two men can do that. No two women can do that. A man and a woman together, the image of God, can do that.

This is the reason that the Bible does not affirm homosexual marriage. Nowhere. Not overtly. Not covertly.

JESUS' OWN WORDS

Over the years I have done nearly 750 interviews with television or radio or in print journalism, many of which involved a discussion of marriage. In some cases, I was in a quasi debate venue. I am amazed at the number of times that the pro-homosexual "marriage" advocates have tried to invoke the name of Jesus as a supporter of homosexuality in general and homosexual "marriage" specifically. Their thinking is fuzzy, muddled, and revisionistic.

The only time Jesus participated in a wedding or spoke of marriage, he referred very specifically to male and female constituents. The classic passage of Matthew 19:4-6 seems to have strangely evaporated from the Bibles of these dull and blinded zealots.

Jesus stated it rather succinctly:

> *Haven't you read... that at the beginning the Creator "made them male and female," and said, "For this reason a man will leave his father and mother and be united to his wife, and the two will become one flesh"? So they are no longer two, but one. Therefore*

what God has joined together, let man not separate (Matthew 19:4-6 NIV).

Note that it says *"for this reason."* For *what* reason? It is because people are "male" and "female"—gender specific, something our liberal friends try hard to deny—that they leave parents and become *one.* Two men together or two women together cannot become one. Only a male and a female can become one. Though not wanting to be indelicate, let me state it clearly: a male "fits" with a female.

And then, just in case there were any in the crowd who were not "getting it"—as some apparently are not today—Jesus explained "one flesh," saying they are "no longer two, but one."

But He didn't stop there (allow me to paraphrase): "What God has labeled as marriage, don't let any judge, legislature, voting group, or even a liberal theologian redefine!" Admittedly this is a loose paraphrase, but it accurately depicts the sternness of Jesus' warning. Briefly stated, He said, "Don't mess with marriage!" And God means it.

He means it because, as we saw in Genesis, "oneness marriage" (that is, male and female) expresses the notion of the image of God. The Bible opens with a marriage between a man and a woman. The Bible closes with a wedding between a groom and bride. In between, the one man-one woman marriage is extolled in both Old and New Testament, as well as by Jesus Himself.

REAL MARRIAGE VERSUS THE IMAGE OF MARRIAGE

Having said that, let's take our understanding of marriage to the next level. Oftentimes, we think that real marriage is what we see here on earth, that of a man and woman. We sometimes assume that God simply "borrowed" the metaphor of marriage in an attempt to describe what will happen in the book of Revelation at the culmination of all history, the marriage of Jesus and the Church. But in reality, we have it backward.

Actually "marriage" on this earth, as wonderful as it is, might be spelled with a small "m." The real Marriage (spelled with a capital "M") is the one at the culmination of history, the Marriage of the Groom (Jesus) and the Bride (the Church).

Thus we have never ever seen the *Real* Marriage. That is yet to come at the end of time. Here on earth, we only have a "shadow" of the real thing. With earthly marriage, we are experiencing merely the hors d'oeuvre, or appetizer, not the main course. God established earthly marriage between a man and a woman to provide a tiny glimpse of the spectacular True Marriage. Intimacy between a married man and woman is only a miniscule glimpse of the breath-taking oneness that Jesus and the Church will experience. Admittedly this marriage between Jesus and the Church is a mystery, a word Paul uses when attempting to describe it (see Eph. 5:31-33). Simply put, this marriage is inexplicable.

I have written a book titled *Heaven and the Afterlife*. When I am interviewed about the book, people often ask, "Why is there no marriage in Heaven? Why is there no sexual expression in Heaven?" The answer may surprise you. There *is* marriage in Heaven! *Real* marriage. *The* marriage. The marriage of the Lamb, Jesus, to the Church. That is real marriage.

Think of the very best marriage you know here on earth. (I hope it is your own marriage.) What is so special about that marriage? The intimacy. The warmth. The joy of being with each other. That is what the Jesus–Church marriage is going to be. Those great marriages on earth are simply to make you long for the *perfect* marriage yet to come.

And what about sex? Not to be indelicate, but the author of Psalm 16 said, *"...at your right hand are pleasures forevermore"* (Ps. 16:11). The ecstasy, the joy of covenantal, marital love-making is a sign of the pleasure to come, the joy of being with Jesus.

I am not trying to be crass when I say that it is not by accident that we use "marital bed" terms to describe the end of history: the "climax" of history, the "consummation" of history. Those have sexual or pleasurable overtones for good reason. We will experience indescribable pleasure as the Church, married to Jesus! It is a mystery, for sure, but it is for real.

If I was the evil one, I would be obsessed with destroying marriage, the coming together and fitting together of the two complementary halves of humanity, male and female, for two reasons:

1. They are on earth as a mirror, the image of God.

2. They are a depiction of what is to be fulfilled at the end of this age in the ultimate Marriage.

And that is why we are in the battle we are in. It is not ultimately about earthly marriage, about our religious freedoms, or even about the practice of homosexuality as such. It is about the desire of satan to decimate the picture of God's ultimate design for the cosmos—the Grand Wedding of His Son to the prepared Bride.

And that is why votes to preserve marriage must remain center stage in our lives. Much is at stake. We need a full, complete "reformation of marriage!" But it must begin with believers understanding these theological underpinnings regarding marriage.

COMMITTING TO MEMORY

I know it is possible to overwhelm people, including you the reader, with too much information. However, there were three things I asked every person to commit to memory:

- The biblical foundation for marriage: Genesis portrays the image of God; Jesus' words; and Revelation portrays the marriage event (as already listed)

- The three political evidences of how same-sex "marriage" would negatively impact traditional marriage (listed next)

- And the ABCs listed (to be discussed later)

In my opinion, a part of experiencing the reformation of marriage is the call for everyone to be able to defend it—succinctly, clearly, persuasively. Contrary to what you might think, that is not hard. Truth is on your side!

DOES GAY MARRIAGE HURT YOUR MARRIAGE?

Over the course of the Prop 8 battle, I was interviewed many times, including four times on *Larry King Live* and the *Dr. Phil Show*. During the first taping of Dr. Phil, he turned to a Christian couple and asked the question that I had heard so many times, "So how does gay marriage hurt your marriage?" The very bright woman who began to respond struggled, understandably, with the question. And so do most people, even strong, mature church people.

Let's answer that question. For starters, when the definition of marriage is changed, it does not change it for just "some"—that is, homosexuals—it changes the definition of marriage for us all. Frankly, it cheapens marriage. That may account for the fact that in Europe, where same-sex "marriage" has been around much longer, after the new "inclusive" laws were enacted, marriage rates plummeted! One would think it might work the other way.

Much has been said about the large numbers of gay people who came to California to get married to their partners, since California was the first state to allow people to come from other states to marry. But the number (considering this was a national "invitation," here referred to as "marriage tourism") was amazingly small. Why? *Because the radical gay agenda is really less about changing the definition of marriage as it is getting you to affirm their lifestyle.*

So back to the key question, "How does gay marriage hurt your marriage?" There are three key illustrations for one major point. The major point is this: Wherever the government has an interest in affirming and protecting gay "marriage," or even gay relations, it has an equal interest in silencing you if you dare speak out against it, even if you are citing Scripture.

The result is loss of parental rights, loss of religious liberties, and loss of personal freedoms. There are countless examples, but I will mention only a few:

Parental rights: David and Tonya Parker's second grader was being taught about homosexuality and homosexual marriage in the Lexington, Massachusetts, public schools. They were prohibited from exercising their legal right to "opt out" their child because (1) "homosexual marriage is now legal so you cannot opt out your child" and (2) "we are teaching homosexuality, not sexuality." The radical homosexual lobby *always* says, in every state battle, "We will not teach it in the schools." Then they promptly teach it in the schools.

- Religious liberties: Sweden provides a historical model for us. Ake Green was arrested, tried, and sentenced to one month in prison for preaching from biblical passages discussing homosexual practice. Much closer to home, the Ocean Grove Camp Meeting Association, one of the nation's oldest and most beautiful, lost the tax exemption on a portion of its property when it refused to perform a ceremony for two lesbians. New Jersey officials contended that since some public funding had been used for that portion of the property, they now had a right to control the policies of this historic, independent Methodist Holiness campground.

- Personal freedoms: Twenty-five-year-old Elaine Huguenin, a photographer from Albuquerque, New Mexico, was fined $6,700 by the state when she refused, for personal, religious reasons, to take pictures of a homosexual commitment ceremony.

There are hundreds more of these types of examples. The key is this: government protection of same-sex relations and "marriage" always results in loss of freedoms and liberties for all people who hold convictions with the scope of historic, orthodox Christianity.

EXPLANATIONS AND DISCLAIMERS

This might be a good time to make some quick disclaimers and explanations:

- There is a distinction between "the nice homosexual who lives next door" and the overtly political, radical gay agenda. Most self-proclaimed homosexuals are nice people and should be treated with respect as people. The "radical gay agenda" is not nice. In fact, it is highly militant and profoundly intolerant, as we learned in California.

- There is no comparison between the civil rights movement of the 1960s and the homosexual demands of today. That is a co-opting of historical reality. As my black friends often say, "I know many ex-homosexuals, but I don't know any ex-blacks." Pigmentation should never be confused with bedroom preference.

- *Sexual orientation,* a rather modern term, is not referred to in the Scriptures. What the Bible addresses are homosexual *actions.* Many people who perceive themselves as being "oriented" homosexually are able to live "above" those inclinations and not give into them.

- Standing for traditional, natural marriage is not "fear-mongering" or "intolerant" or "hateful." Do not be bullied by those who try to take away your: (1) biblical convictions, (2) your right to free speech on this topic, and (3) your right to carry your convictions into the voting booth.

- The reason that there is a 2 percent to 10 percent swing between polling and actual voting in state after state on this topic is because many people *are* bullied and threatened on the topic; thus, they act like they support same-sex "marriage" until they get in the safe privacy of the voting booth.

- Do not "buy into" the two key words of the radical gay movement, the two "I" words: (1)

intimidation and (2) inevitability, the belief that it is "inevitable" that they will win in the plans to redefine and destroy marriage. They have said it was "inevitable" for 20 years, yet 31 states have voted on this, with all 31 voting for traditional, natural marriage. Nearly seven out of ten Americans believe in natural marriage.

- This issue is not rocket science. Nature teaches that the man that produces the sperm and the woman who produces the egg are, in most cases, best suited to raise the child. If not them, then the facsimile of a mother and a father are the best alternative.

- Since marriage *is* historically, in part, about procreation, those advocating same sex "marriages" are saying that either a mother is unimportant or a father is unimportant. Which one, I ask you, is unimportant?

FROM AUDIENCE 1 TO AUDIENCE 2

We return to the historical components of this story. As noted earlier, if we were going to see the "reformation of marriage" during the California Prop 8 battle, we needed access to thousands of lay-people. Evening satellite simulcasts were launched, involving some 300 locations across the state, down linked for audiences gathered in each venue.

In September and October 2008, tightly scripted 90-minute live presentations were uplinked and then down linked into 300 auditoriums across the state. Once again, the goal of these productions was to equip the average layperson to be able to articulate the key issues regarding the defense of marriage without quoting a single Bible verse, but rather drawing on data from social science.

We refer to the Church audience as "Audience #1." They need to know the Word of God regarding marriage. However, we want the "first audience" to also know social science that confirms the advantage and necessity for marriage so that they can communicate truth to the unchurched, which we see as "Audience #2." The chart below demonstrates this, along with the use of media which was twofold:

- To activate believers

- To educate the unchurched

To do this, we developed memorable, alphabetized talking points, letters "A" through "J." "A" through "F" were for the churched to be able to share with the unchurched. Letters "G" through "J" were for believers to be able to share with other believers. Known as "The ABCs of Restoring and Protecting Marriage," they are:

A. **Anti-Family Laws, Activist Judges, and Over-reaching Legislators** (the democracy issue): We need to *restore* to the people what *anti-family* government officials have taken away. Otherwise we will have a legislative/judicial oligarchy (a small group, not the people, rules).

B. **Benefits** (the political issue): Many states have already given to same-sex couples *all* the *benefits* a state can give, *but* the demand to redefine the word *marriage* is going too far.

C. **Children** (the family issue): Since the public schools teach information about the "family," children as young as kindergarten will be taught about homosexuality and marriage. This creates *confusion* in *children*.

D. **Dads and Moms** (the family issue): Every child *needs* and *deserves* a daddy and a mommy.

E. **Everywhere** (the sociological issue): First, every part of the world has affirmed heterosexual, monogamous marriage as the healthy *building block* of society, whether pre-Christian, Christian, or non-Christian. There is a reason for this: it works. Second, in countries where same-sex marriage is now occurring, marriage rates have plummeted. Third, now that the definition of marriage has been changed, some groups are already attempting to legalize polygamy. Other bizarre forms will follow.

F. **Freedoms** (the liberty issue): In countries where same-sex "marriage" is legalized, people (especially pastors) are being fined and tried if they affirm one-man-one-woman marriage, object to homosexual "marriage," or cite the Bible regarding the practice of homosexuality. It has now begun in this country. Religious freedom is at stake. Pastors will eventually be forced to perform same-sex weddings or be fined or go to jail.

NOTE: A through F are for sharing with unbelievers, the unchurched, or people who are biblically unaware. G through J can be added when believers are sharing with other believers.

G. **God** (the theological issue): God said "one man and one woman." Only the most bizarre twisting of the Bible can interpret it any other way. *Historic, orthodox Christianity* has affirmed one-man-one-woman marriage for 2,000 years. Judeo-Christian culture and other cultures have affirmed it for 5,000 years. The United States has affirmed heterosexual marriage since its inception in 1776. California has affirmed it for 158 years.

H. **Homosexual Practices** (compassion and transformational issue): First, we love all people. We hate no one. To disagree with someone is *not* to hate them. Do not be bullied on this issue. Homosexuals should be and are loved. Second, since the *act* or *practice* of homosexuality is a choice, they can be transformed by the power of the Holy Spirit. There is overwhelming evidence of people who have received the power of God on their lives and have been transformed.

I. **I must be involved** in praying, talking, telephoning, and door-to-door teams.

J. **Jesus Is the Answer**: We do not make an "idol" of marriage. Jesus is the issue.

PART 2:
ACTIVATION

By way of review, our long-term strategy consisted of:

- Communication

- Activation

- Prayer

We now shift our discussion from Communication to Activation.

GROUND TROOPS

In addition to the conference calls, the phone campaign, and the satellite simulcasts, there was another component in the ground war. We encouraged all churches that would to set up phone banks. We trained their phone callers online to call all people within their data bank, since the computer systems in most churches have approximately four to five times more names than the weekly average attendance in weekend services. Nearly 300 churches joined in this endeavor.

Brilliant strategists laid out a grassroots door-to-door campaign that would call for 64,000 people to go house-to-house—40 volunteers for each of the 1,600 California zip codes targeted by the effort. Although the goal of 64,000 was not reached during this portion of the campaign, increasing numbers were being trained for the big November 4 election day push for 100,000 people. Perhaps as many as 8 million of the state's 16 million registered voters received a knock at their door, with another 4 million receiving a phone call. Three-fourths of California's registered voters were contacted, which helped them grasp the nature of marriage. This accomplishment was one of the key facets of the entire campaign—totally stunning the "no on 8" advocates, who had no comparable campaign.

EXPECTING PERSECUTION

But those against God's definition of marriage rebelled against this "reformation of marriage." The animosity from the anti-marriage objectors heightened through such things as hate mail, intimidation, and bullying. Acts of violence and vandalism were evidenced all over the state. Many Bible-believing pastors and churches beefed up security. One pastor had police protection due to constant threats against his life. Some people were assaulted and many church facilities were vandalized. This did not deter the courageous "yes on 8" advocates in the slightest.

FINANCES

In addition to massive door-knocking and telephoning campaigns, people gave sacrificially to this grand "reformation of marriage" campaign. Some $42 million was given for the signature gather phase and the Prop 8 campaign.

PART 3:
PRAYER

You may recall that I said our God-given strategy consisted of:

- Communication—establishing truth in the hearts of people

- Activation—calling on people to knock on doors, to call on the telephone, and to talk

- Prayer—40 days of fast, culminating in a 12-hour prayer meeting

A FORTY-DAY FAST

At this point, the prayer campaign begun earlier ramped up. Tens of thousands of Californians began a 40-day fast on September 24, leading up to the election on November 3. Many fasted from solid foods, having only a liquid diet, while others fasted one or two meals a day. A team of about 40 young adults converged in San Diego from all over the nation to not merely fast, but to pray from 6 A.M. to 11 P.M. every day, all day, for six days a week, taking only Sundays off. Several times the group switched from the 6 A.M. to 11 P.M. prayer schedule to praying 24 hours a day, sometimes three days at a time, and fasting from all solid and liquid foods, relying on water only as they looked to God to answer their prayers for California. At the end of the fast, they actually fasted from water, too, for three days!

On Saturday, November 1, 2008, 33,000 people gathered for 12 hours of intense prayer in Qualcomm Stadium in San Diego, praying out loud for most of the 12 hours with great intensity. It was webcast; consequently people joined in the prayer meeting from all over the world.

SUMMARY: ELECTION DAY

In prayer and action, faith and works truly merged. Tuesday November 4 produced the biggest grassroots effort ever executed in U.S. political history. The only thing that might have compared previously was the marriage vote in Ohio in 2004, but that is a considerably smaller state, both in geography and in population. A massive "Get Out the Vote" Plan came to fruition as 100,000 people activated across the state. With nearly 21,000 precincts in the state, the goal of a team of five—one captain and four workers—per precinct was virtually realized that day.

Another evidence of victory was felt when the Amendment 2 Florida vote—three hours earlier than California—was victorious at 62 percent (60 percent was needed to add it to the Constitution). Arizona's Prop 102, in the same time zone, had results fairly early, handily passing as well.[2] This encouraged Californians that victory was near.

At approximately 11:45 P.M. on election night, Frank Schubert, the political brains of the Prop 8 battle, officially "called" the campaign a victory. His colleague Jeff Flint had confirmed by computer models that the "no on 8" vote could not win, and "yes" had clearly and indisputably won. The 11:45 P.M. moment was special. A mighty shout went up on the 17th floor of the Westgate Hotel, where many of us had gathered. Many wept and embraced. Then it hit us! God had done this. We stopped shouting victory and went right to prayer and began praising, worshiping, and thanking God!

The victory was solid. In the end, the measure passed by a solid 52.3 percent to 47.7 percent. The official statement of the vote, according to the California Secretary of State, shows that Proposition 8 won by a margin of 600,000 votes: 7,001,084 to 6,401,483.[3] The majority had spoken. Twice. Once through Prop 22 in 2000, and now through Prop 8 in 2008. People had worked hard to preserve natural marriage. God had interceded. Marriage and society itself had won a decisive and important victory. A "reformation of marriage" had begun.

This is only one state's story. Your state has a story. As of November 2009, 31 states have voted on the definition of marriage. All 31 have voted in favor of traditional, biblical, natural marriage, Maine being the most recent to stand for marriage in a stunning, and from the left, unexpected, 53 percent to 47 percent victory.[4]

But reformations are not founded primarily or at least exclusively in voting booths. Reformations are fanned in the hearts of people. Thus, the battle continues. We fasted 40 days to see (1) Prop 8 pass and (2) the hearts of Californians to long for righteousness. We have seen the first. We await the revival that will spark the second.

As we see this reformation continue, the "image of God" is being preserved on the earth. The "mystery" of the Marriage of the Lamb is being maintained. Truly, we are watching, and experiencing—or at least beginning to experience—a reformation of marriage.

Chapter 7

STOPPING FOR THE ONE

HEIDI BAKER

Pledge 7: I will fight racism and social injustice, care for God's planet, and do all that I can to eradicate systemic poverty through my sphere of influence (see Matt. 6:9-13).

When the Son of Man comes in His glory and all His angels are with Him, He will sit on His glorious throne. The people of every nation will be gathered in front of Him. He will separate them as a shepherd separates the sheep from the goats. He will put the sheep on His right but the goats on His left. Then the king will say to those on His right, "Come, My Father has blessed you! Inherit the kingdom prepared for you from the creation of the world. I was hungry, and you gave Me something to eat. I was thirsty, and you gave Me something to drink. I was a stranger, and you took Me into your home. I needed clothes, and you gave Me something to wear. I was sick, and you took care of Me. I was in prison, and you visited Me." Then the people who have God's approval will reply to Him, "Lord, when did we see You hungry and feed You or see You thirsty and give You something to drink? When did we see You as a stranger and take You into our homes or see You in need of clothes and give You something to wear? When did we see You sick or in prison and visit You?" The king will answer them, "I can guarantee this truth: Whatever you did for one of My brothers or sisters, no matter how unimportant [they seemed], you did for Me." Then the king will say to those on His left, "Get away from Me! God has cursed you! Go into everlasting fire that was prepared for the devil and his angels! I was hungry, and you gave me nothing to eat. I was thirsty, and you gave Me nothing to drink. I was a stranger, and you didn't take Me into your homes. I needed clothes, and you didn't give Me anything to wear. I was sick and in prison, and you didn't take care of Me." They, too, will ask, "Lord, when did we see You hungry or thirsty or as a stranger or in need of clothes or sick or in prison and didn't help You?" He will answer them, "I can guarantee this truth: Whatever you failed to do for one of My brothers or sisters, no matter how unimportant [they seemed], you failed to do for Me."' These people will go away into eternal punishment, but those with God's approval will go into eternal life (Matthew 25:31-46 GWT).

Over the years, many have debated the answers to questions about the eradication of social injustice and systemic poverty. I believe that for over 2,000 years we have had the answer and the blueprint because our King Jesus holds the solution to every problem on the planet, no matter how enormous! And as His ambassadors, we partner with Him to release these answers to society to bring about historic change. We are called to walk out the very ideas and thoughts of Heaven here on earth. As stewards of the earth and carriers of glory, we can fearlessly bring God's solution to floods, famines, and epidemics. We are called to reform the earth by releasing Heaven.

I believe that the answer to these complicated questions is found in Matthew 25. Here, Jesus shows us the key to overcoming some of the world's greatest challenges. The King of glory says, *"Come, you who are blessed of My Father! Inherit the kingdom prepared for you..."* (Matt. 25:34). As lovers and followers of Jesus, we desire to be blessed by the Father and to receive our inheritance, which is to see the Kingdom of Heaven advancing on earth! This is our mandate, to release His Kingdom on earth as it is in Heaven (see Matt. 6:10).

What does it look like for the Kingdom of Heaven to be released here on earth? We know that in Heaven there are no children dying of starvation, no widows left alone with no one to care for them, no old ladies living in a cage as sex slaves. In Heaven there is no famine, no abandonment, and no sex trade. There is no systemic poverty. There is no racism. There is no social injustice. God's powerful love wipes it all out! This is the Kingdom reality that we are called to release.

DO WE HAVE EYES TO SEE HIM?

The Lord Himself explains to us, with striking simplicity, what this reality looks like:

I was hungry, and you gave Me something to eat. I was thirsty, and you gave Me something to drink. I was a stranger, and you took Me into your home. I needed clothes, and you gave Me something to wear. I was sick, and you took care of Me. I was in prison, and you visited Me (Matthew 25:35-36 GWT).

Jesus says "I was hungry." **He** was hungry.

Every human on the planet is created in the image of God, every single one, without exception. When we look at anyone, we should be able to see the fingerprint of God in that person. His very image is stamped on each one. This may be a challenge for some of us when we look at the drunk beggar asking us for money as we hurry along the road or when we turn on the television and see images of a child in a dump covered in dirt, scabs, and worms.

However, we all need to ask ourselves this crucial question: How do we look at broken humanity? How do we look at starving, dying people? Are they just a project? Are they only a problem that needs fixing? Do we care about their existence or see them at all? Do we even want to see them? It is all too easy for many of us to simply change the television channel or turn off the radio when we are confronted with uncomfortable news about the suffering of humanity. However, when we do this, we are turning away from our very own brothers and sisters who are in great need. In that moment, we forget that they are truly created in the image of God.

COURAGE TO SEE BEAUTY

It's often easier to see the negative in others and focus on their faults and weakness. It takes a lot more faith and courage to find the beauty. I decided awhile ago that I was going to find the beauty in every human whom I face each day, that I was going to find the image of God in every man, woman, and child with whom I come in contact. I am determined to make this my priority, no matter what comes my way. Even though this can take effort and courage, it is the direction I choose to set my heart in. I want to see the Kingdom of God break forth. I want to see His Kingdom in each person every day.

Jesus has renewed my mind, and now I think differently. When I see pain, tragedy, and disease, I look beyond the suffering into the eyes of the dying person before me, and I know that I am looking into the eyes of my Savior! I am looking into the eyes of my King, into the eyes of the One I love!

My mind is no longer the mind of a natural woman from my privileged background of Laguna Beach, California. I have been transformed. Neither AIDS nor poverty scares me any longer. I see situations like these as opportunities for the passion and power of Christ Jesus to defeat satan and release God's Kingdom love to bring transformation.

We see a lot of suffering and poverty and face great need here in Mozambique every single day. But Jesus has changed the way I think so that, if I ever feel overwhelmed by the enormous need in front of me, I simply look into His eyes, and I am reminded that there will always be enough because He died. I know who my God is! This fills me with courage to once again look into the eyes of the one dying child, the one broken man, the one lonely widow and determine to love them into the Kingdom. I no longer wonder how we are going to build the next house or how we are going to feed yet another child.

When we have the mind of Christ and really begin to understand that the suffering, broken people whom we are looking at or hearing about, are brothers and sisters created in the image of our Father, not stopping is no longer an option! Not giving food when we see them starving becomes impossible! We cannot turn away from those we see suffering because we cannot turn away from Jesus! We cannot close our eyes to them because we cannot close our eyes to Him!

WE CAN ALL DO SOMETHING

...I was thirsty and you gave Me drink..." (Matthew 25:35).

Jesus said, "*I* was thirsty and *you* gave me something to drink." Who is Jesus talking about? He's talking about you! *You* gave Him something to drink. So what does it look like for Jesus to be thirsty? It looks like our brothers and sisters, created in the image of God, suffering with thirst for lack of clean water. It looks like the village I went to today—a village filled with thousands of people living in mud huts without running water, electricity, medical care, or schooling. This village was full of children in rags with bloated bellies who have to walk over an hour (one way) in the scorching heat to get to the only hand-pumped, fresh water well available. I saw a huge queue of people waiting for hours just to pump a container of water. Imagine having to do this every day! Imagine what this is like when you have a family of six young children and you can only carry one container of water on your head at a time. One hour there and one hour back! That's why no child had clean clothes. They only had crusty, black rags to wear. This was thirst staring us in the face! How do we respond to this thirst?

If we want to eradicate the injustice and suffering of systemic poverty, then we literally have to see through the eyes of this verse: that Jesus Himself is asking *us* for a drink. What a difference it would make if every church on the planet drilled a well. There are thousands of churches here in Mozambique that are longing for fresh water wells so that people can come from surrounding villages to drink, not only physical, but also spiritual water. Just earlier today, we were drilling for fresh water at our Village of Joy children's center in Pemba, Mozambique. It will be such a beautiful, joyful sight when we hit water. It will mean that thousands of people will be able to come from the surrounding areas to drink fresh water. It will mean that the thirst of Jesus will be quenched once again!

> ...*I was a stranger and you took Me in* (Matthew 25:35).

When every one of us begins to see the poor as our family, and not just as numbers, statistics, projects, or problems that need fixing, reformation will come to society. As lovers of Jesus, we are called to mirror the values and reality of Heaven here on earth. We are called to have eyes to see our brothers and sisters in need and ears to hear their cries for help! The Lord is not asking for everyone to do huge things. But He is asking that we all do something! For example, we can all sponsor at least one child, even if we are not able to take care of an entire family right now. But there is no reason that we should shut our eyes and walk by our brothers and sisters who are in desperate need. The Church is called to lead the way in living a life of radical love toward our neighbors, not to simply turn away in judgment or indifference from the cries of the poor, broken, and oppressed.

WHO IS MY NEIGHBOR?

You may ask "Who is my neighbor?" In Luke 10:25-37, an expert of the religious laws of the day asked Jesus the very same question. He believed he had already lived according to all of God's requirements: loving God with all your heart, soul, strength, and mind and loving your neighbor as yourself (see Luke 10:28). So he asked this question in order to justify himself.

However, Jesus saw that something vital was missing in this young man's devotional life! Jesus responded by telling the young "expert" a story about one suffering man who was left to die on the side of the road because he had been robbed and beaten nearly to death. First a priest (a religious man) and then a Levite (a worshiper) passed by this dying man with complete indifference. Then a Samaritan man (of mixed race and held in contempt at the time) saw him and stopped for him! In compassion, he poured out his time, energy, and resources to nurse the brother whom he had never even met back to health.

This is the man, Jesus says, who was a true neighbor—the one who had mercy, the one who had eyes to see the one dying man on the side of the road, the one who chose to let himself be inconvenienced as he hurried along the road, the one who stopped and had compassion, the one who chose love!

Our neighbor might not literally live next door to us or even in the same country; our neighbor is simply the one the Lord lets us see or hear about each day. Whether it's as we pass them by in the mall or as we hear about them on the news, we need to have eyes to see that each suffering brother or sister needs a *true* neighbor to see them and to stop for them. If every believer on the planet took care of at least one brother or one sister in need, no one would ever need to die of starvation again! If every believer took care of just one and provided for them financially and prayed for them, it would look like reformation. It would look like the revival of love that we have been praying for and longing to see. Revival does have a face and love does look like something. It's as simple as every single believer caring for the one. It is so incredibly simple that it is easy to miss! We look, we stop, and we love—every day!

CEASELESS, LIMITLESS, BOTTOMLESS LOVE

The Gospel is about love. It is about sacrificial love that sometimes feels like inconvenience. It is the kind of love that disrupts our day. The kind of love that hurts! This love that is ceaseless, limitless, and bottomless is our only mandate in life! It is our only ambition and our greatest joy! My personal resume is about love. My title is lover. My calling is to love, to live so deeply inside the heart of my God that I am able to love my neighbor well—even if he is mean or he smells and is oozing with sores!

When you live inside the heart of God and are continually filled with His love, you are no longer concerned about the cost of stopping and loving. You are only concerned about the treasure of Christ Jesus and the treasure of the one dying man on the road in front of you. You are no longer concerned about numbers and how many people you can say you are feeding or the size of your meetings and conferences. You are only concerned about hearing the heartbeat of your King. You are only concerned about looking into the face of Jesus and looking into the face of the one in front of you and feeling the love, compassion, and mercy of God flowing through you. My life is summed up in this: passion and compassion—passion for Jesus and compassion for my neighbor.

Jesus Himself sees us and stops for us. Now we must be compelled by love to fearlessly run into the darkest and most poverty-stricken places of the earth and to pour out the wine and oil of the Kingdom upon the wounds of this broken world one person at a time!

REVIVAL HAS A FACE

I was naked and you clothed Me... (Matthew 25:36).

Yesterday a group of poor village children came to visit me in my office. They had just been to our children's program, where they had eaten and learned about Jesus. They came in wearing shredded shirts that looked like rags so I gave them clothes to take home. The Kingdom of God looks like something and revival has a face! It's the face of simple love in action! If you see someone in shredded rags and you have two shirts, then give them one! I believe that if you love Christ Jesus and call yourself His, then you will not be able to close your eyes when you see someone naked or dressed in rags. But you will offer them what you have out of the abundance that God has given you.

It does not take a science degree to figure out that a child dressed in rags needs a new shirt! And yet the truth of simple obedience to practical love is overlooked every day as we spend time going to church growth seminars and look for the latest teaching on how to get breakthrough for our churches and in our society! Many don't realize that we already have the answer! We already have the blueprint to reformation. We have the book. Now we just need to live it!

It is so simple that everyone can do it. No one is excluded. Everyone can love. Everyone has something to give. The poor widow in Elisha's day only had one small jar of oil and a handful of flour. She was so poor that she was preparing for her own and her child's funeral! Self-preservation would have us hold on to our last little bit of food. And yet, in an outrageous act of worship, the widow gave away the little she had left. In great faith, she offered her tiny meal to God, and He couldn't resist such an extravagant act of love. Throughout the rest of the famine, neither her flour nor her oil stopped flowing! (See First Kings 17:8-16.)

WE NEED TO GROW DOWN

Every day I choose again to yield to the heart of Jesus and hear it beating with love for the poor and suffering. I choose to surrender to the breaking and the compassion of His heart flowing through me so that His light can be irresistible in this dark world. Jesus gave everything away for love's sake, and my worship back to God is to give all that I am and all that I have to Him! My desire is to glorify the Father through an obedient, laid down life of love! I offer up my little life to Jesus every day.

I learn about the Kingdom from children because they don't complicate things the way adults do. The little boy in John 6 only had a small packed lunch (two *small* fish and five barley loaves of bread). There were 5,000 starving men in the crowd, as well as many women and children! Jesus was testing the disciples' faith and asked them where they could buy bread to feed the hungry crowd (see John 6:5). One of the disciples, Andrew, voiced the feeling many of us often have when we are faced with great need, *"How far will they go among so many?"* (John 6:9 NIV). Maybe he was concerned that, if the little they had was given away, there would be nothing left to satisfy his own hunger!

However, the little child didn't seem to be of the same mind as Andrew, and despite the obvious odds, he offered up his little lunch to Jesus. And he got the incredible joy of seeing Jesus multiply his little offering to the hungry crowd right in front of His eyes! Many of us want to have this same joy, and we pray for the multiplication of finances and provision. We wonder why nothing happens, but we forget that we must first put something into the hands of God before we can see Him multiply it! Are we prepared to release the little that we have to feed the hungry brother? We need to grow down, become more like this little child, and start giving our little lunch away in love.

Jesus is calling us to be more like the widow and the little boy. He is calling us to move in radical, prophetic acts of love and mercy that the world has never seen before! He is inviting us to offer up our little lives to Him and to live surrendered, holy, given, laid-down lives of love.

LOVING THE POOR IS PART OF OUR WORSHIP

Loving the poor and the broken is part of our worship to Jesus. If we say we love Jesus, then we love the poor. If we say we love Jesus, then we love the hungry. If we say we love Jesus, then we love the thirsty. If we say we love Jesus, then we care for the orphan. If we say we love Jesus, we care for the strangers, and we see them housed. If we say we love Jesus, we clothe the naked and those in rags. If we say we love Jesus, we take the time to visit the sick in the hospital, and when we can, we even build the hospitals. We pray for the sick and the hurting because we care about their pain. We never stop loving!

> ...*I was in prison and you came to Me* (Matthew 25:36).

There isn't a place in the world without a prison. If every Christian committed to visiting a prisoner, even just once a year, there would be no prisoner left without a visit! There would no longer be any prisoners left alone, and they would be transformed by the love of God. Mercy is not complicated. Jesus is simply asking us to stop for the one because then we are stopping for Him!

MINISTERING TO JESUS

> *Then the righteous will answer Him, "Lord, when did we see You hungry and feed You or thirsty and give You something to drink?"* (Matthew 25:37 NIV)

Some of you reading this may be having the same bewildered reaction as those, in this parable, who had gained God's approval. They didn't understand what Jesus was saying or how it could be so simple! When did they minister to the Lord Himself?

They may have thought that they never saw Jesus with a bloated belly or hungry on the garbage dump, eating rubbish, even though they fed the dying child under the tree and opened feeding programs. They didn't recall seeing Jesus thirsty as they drilled wells and shared water with people who were hurting and dying. They didn't remember seeing Jesus as a stranger and inviting Him in. They just remember housing a child that had no home and building them a mud hut. They never saw Jesus needing clothes. They only remember giving their outgrown children's clothing to those who had none. They went to the hospital and visited people in the AIDS wards, but they didn't see Jesus there! They visited the mentally ill and prayed for them. They visited Alzheimer's homes and talked to the elderly who didn't even know that they were there or even when they came or left. They didn't see Jesus in prison as they sat with the prisoners and told them that they were loved and not forgotten and that they were forgiven because of the cross.

WHATEVER YOU DID FOR
THE LEAST OF THESE

The king will reply, "I tell you the truth: Whatever you did for one of the least of these brothers [or sisters] of mine [no matter how unimportant they seemed], you did for Me" (Matthew 25:40 NIV).

However, Jesus answered them that as they ministered to the least and seemingly the most unimportant ones that they came across, they ministered to Him! It is only here on earth that we have an opportunity to bring pleasure to Jesus by seeing Him, by faith, in the poor and broken. In Heaven it will be easy to love Jesus when we see Him in all His glory, but here on earth we have the incredible privilege of loving Jesus when He comes to us disguised in a cloak of hunger, thirst, poverty, and need.

The message of this parable is so startling that it would be simpler to skip over! But this truth is unavoidable! *"Whatever you did for one of the least of these, you did for Me."* This is something that ought to convict everyone who goes by the name of Christian and says that they are a follower of Christ Jesus.

DO YOU KNOW ME?

Then he will say to those on his left, "Depart from me, you who are cursed, into the eternal fire prepared for the devil and his angels. For I was hungry and you gave me nothing to eat, I was thirsty and you gave me nothing to drink, I was a stranger and you did not invite me in, I needed clothes and you did not clothe me, I was sick and in prison and you did not look after me" (Matthew 25:41-43 NIV).

In this incredible statement Jesus is saying that if you do not care for the poor, you do not know Him! This is not a special calling or something for just one sweet, little person with a special gift of compassion. This is not for super Christians or followers of Mother Theresa only. This is for every single person on the planet who calls himself or herself a follower of Christ! Jesus is literally saying to those on the left, "Depart from Me. If you did not care for the poor, if you did not stop for the one, if you did not feed the hungry, if you did not give a drink to the thirsty, then you don't know Me!"

Our cities are full of those who are homeless, those who are mentally ill, drug addicts, and alcoholics. We need to see them, stop for them, and take care of them. There are millions of homeless people living under trees or in cardboard boxes, in desperate need of shelter. There are pregnant teenagers who would keep their children if they only knew that they were loved and could be taken into families. If only they knew that they would be cared for, nurtured, and prayed for! If only there was someone who would show them the mercy and grace of God and would be willing to stop for them and be Jesus to them in their loneliness and pain.

Sometimes our ideas don't portray the love of Jesus! For example, we think that if we just picket at the abortion clinic, then we are doing something great for God's Kingdom! But His Kingdom looks like inviting that pregnant, scared teenager to live in our house. If we only picket at the clinic, then the Lord is going to say to us that we did not invite *Him* in when *He* needed a home. In this parable Jesus is saying, "*I* was a stranger. *I* was homeless. *I* was hungry, and *You* didn't take me in. *You* didn't care for Me!"

WAKE UP, CHURCH!

We need to wake up, Church, and start to care for the poor! We need to wake up and grow crops and develop strategies for greater farming technology. We need to wake up and create ways to drill wells all over the world for people who are literally dying because there's no fresh water or who are spending many hours walking just to get enough to survive. Wells give opportunities for productivity. Crop growth brings in provision and income, which in turn gives children prospects for education. Jesus is giving us opportunities to partner with Him, to give our brothers and sisters a hope and a future. True love empowers! We are called to love the poor until their lives are so transformed that they are able to empower those around them.

FIGHTING RACISM

He will reply, "I tell you the truth, whatever you did not do for one of the least of these, you did not do for me" (Matthew 25:45 NIV).

When Jesus said that you didn't visit Him, clothe Him, or give Him water, He was literally saying that you don't know Him. If we want the friendship of God, we need to be friends with those who are poor and broken. We need to see their value and understand that there is no one lesser or higher because of their education, skin color, or social background. When we discriminate and treat one of our brothers differently for any of those reasons, we are literally mistreating Jesus Himself! If we struggle to love those of another race or are scared of other cultures, we simply need to spend time with them and find out that we are all family. We come from the same Father and are all created equally valuable in His eyes. We need to spend time with our brothers and sisters and get to know Christ as we get to know them.

LOVE THAT EMPOWERS

As we help the poor practically, we also need to empower them and restore their dignity so that they can believe in their destinies and be released into all that the Father has dreamed for their lives! At our children's centers, we celebrate every child so that they know how special they are. Many of them don't know their birth dates so they simply choose a date and we make that day their birthday. At these birthday parties, we look every child in the eyes and tell them that the day they were born was a great day and that God is thrilled with their lives and destinies. We tell them that the Lord has created them in His image and that they are beautiful! We tell each one that they can do absolutely anything that's in their hearts! We want them to believe, not only in Jesus, but also in themselves so that they can come into all that they were created to be!

An important key to reversing the curse of systemic poverty is calling the poor to understand the value and beauty of who they are. We need to call them to believe in their destinies. It's not enough to only give people some bread to temporarily relieve their hunger and suffering. We also need to build the bakeries and train them to bake bread for themselves and their families. We need to train them to sell the bread so that they can provide jobs and education to those in their communities! We need to empower the poor to work, study, and train others. We need to think beyond weeklong ministry trips. Child sponsorship needs to be long term. It needs to go beyond keeping children from hunger and starvation today, to empowering them through schooling, vocational training, and even university degrees.

There are people to whom God has given Heaven's blueprints and strategies to care for His planet and develop the economy. With divine wisdom and understanding, they drill and maintain wells, plant supernaturally fruitful crops, and have success in micro-enterprising in third world nations. He gives them plans to build schools with incentives and training programs that empower the poor to provide for their communities! I believe that God has blessed every person on the planet with a powerful gift; it may even be the ability to get breakthroughs in medical research, such as cures to AIDS or malaria. Whatever part we have to play, the eradication of systemic poverty and social injustice should be the concern of every single believer.

HEARING HIS HEARTBEAT

The Lord is calling His Body to hear the heartbeat of the Father for the poor, the lost, and the broken. He is calling each one of us to care for His lost children. And as every one of us stops for even the one person, no one will be left starving under a tree, no one will be left dying in the garbage dump, no one will be left alone. I pray that Jesus reduces us all to this one thing: *love*. Then we can live lives of simplicity, passion for Him, and compassion for our neighbors. This is my only message in life; this is my only desire. I long to be so united with the heart of Jesus that I take on His very nature. I want to move in so much tenderness and so much kindness that I become an irresistible light in this dark world.

The eyes of Jesus are filled with passion and compassion, and He always stops for the one. I want to mirror His rhythm here on earth. I want to carry His fragrance and be so full of Him that when the poor look into my eyes, they see Jesus Himself looking back at them.

The Lord is longing and looking for willing vessels of love, those whom He can fully occupy. He is looking for jars of clay to fully possess with His glory. I believe that Jesus is raising up a whole army, a generation, of radical, servant lovers who are willing to drink of the cup of suffering, as well as the cup of joy, for loves' sake. They will see as He sees, do what He does, and weep as He weeps. These reformers will run fearlessly into the places of greatest need and move in extravagant acts of kindness, mercy, and love that will turn the world upside down! And as God's ceaseless, bottomless, endless love flows through their little lives, fully given, His glory will cover the earth as the waters cover the seas!

Chapter 8

THE SEVEN MOUNTAIN MANDATE

LANCE WALLNAU

Pledge 8: I will discover which of the seven mountains of culture (religion, family, business, government, education, the media, and arts and entertainment). God has designed me to climb, and I will do my part to bring sustained social transformation to those areas to which I am called (see Matt. 28:18-20).

THE SEVEN MOUNTAIN MANDATE

My first encounter with the revelation of the seven mountains of culture goes back to a conversation I had with Loren Cunningham in the year 2000. Loren is the esteemed founder of Youth With A Mission (YWAM), a global missionary organization with an emphasis on enlisting young people in the call to serve Jesus. He shared how, in 1975, he was praying about how to turn the world around for Jesus and saw seven areas. He said, "I saw that we were to focus on these categories to turn around nations to God. I wrote them down and stuck the paper in my pocket."

This was his list:

1. Church

2. Family

3. Education

4. Government and law

5. Media (television, radio, newspaper, Internet)

6. Arts, entertainment, sports

7. Commerce, science, and technology

The day after this revelation, he had a divine appointment. As he put it, "I met with a dear brother, Dr. Bill Bright, leader of Campus Crusade for Christ. He shared with me how God had given him a message, and he felt he needed to share it with me. God had identified areas to concentrate on to turn the nations back to Him! They were the same areas with different wording. Bill was stunned when I took the same notes out of my pocket and showed them to him."

As I heard Loren tell me this story, I was somewhat stunned. It seemed odd that this message had been out since 1974, yet I had not heard about it earlier. It so transformed my thinking that I have made it central to my message ever since. Loren called these seven areas "mind molders," and Bill Bright called them "world kingdoms." I saw them as seven mountains whose lofty heights are mind molders with strongholds that occupy influence as world kingdoms. Each of the seven mountains represents an individual sphere of influence that shapes the way people think. These mountains are crowned with high places that modern-day kings occupy as ideological strongholds. These strongholds are, in reality, houses built out of thoughts. These thought structures are fortified with spiritual reinforcement that shapes the culture and establishes the spiritual climate of each nation. I sensed the Lord telling me, "He who can take these mountains can take the harvest of nations."

Loren felt that the strategy to take the seven mountains would be very straightforward. In *Making Jesus Lord,* he writes:

> First, we take territory from satan in the place of prayer, with the power of the Holy Spirit, through the mighty weapons available to us. We know that spiritual warfare involves pulling down strongholds of false reasoning. We pray against the enemy's influence in whatever area we are aware. Our prayers should be specific. Listening to the Holy Spirit in our minds, He will tell us how to pray. Regional and local matters should be part of our specific focus.

> Second, after we have prayed for a specific sphere of influence, be it government, a school system, an area of the media, or whatever, God may then choose to use us in the very sphere for which we have been praying. He may call us to penetrate that influential place for Him, placing us, like Daniel or Joseph, in a place of authority.[1]

I agree with Loren that our strategy must include spiritual intervention from our position of authority within the Church, as well as influence from our position of authority in the marketplace. In order to take the seven mountains of culture for Christ's Kingdom, we must understand the interaction between the Church, the Gospel, and the culture. An idea I heard a few years ago clarifies this division. There are only four ways we can approach this mission:

1. The Church preaches the Gospel, but is separated from culture:

   Church + Gospel – Culture = Fundamentalism

2. The Church is gathering for social causes, but not preaching the Gospel:

   Church – Gospel + Culture = Liberalism

3. The Gospel is being preached and the culture embraced, but not by the Church:

   Gospel + Culture – Church = Para Church

4. All three are lined up:

   Church + Gospel + Culture = Kingdom

We really don't have a choice in the matter. Without all three: Church, Gospel, and culture, we will fail to change the world in any permanent way. It will require nothing less than the government of God to dispossess and occupy the territory dominated by the gates of hell. This is a supernatural commission that requires the Holy Spirit and spiritual authority to pull off. Some things can be done by casual fellowship, like sipping coffee at Starbucks, but this is not one of them. We need to see the words *"...I will build My church, and the gates of Hades shall not prevail against it"* (Matt. 16:18) in a fresh light. The Church needs to expand its vision of what it takes to *"make disciples of all the nations"* (Matt. 28:19).

LOST GOSPEL, LOST KINGS

As part of my seven mountain journey, I interviewed a key Washington leader who is often referred to as the "stealth Billy Graham" because of his influence behind the scenes with leaders of nations and foreign governments. Out of respect for him, I will leave his name anonymous.

I had not even shaken his hand when he at once set me up with this question: "Who were the people groups God assigned to the apostle Paul? To whom was he sent to preach?"

My mind raced because I knew it was a trick question. *If I say Jews, he may say Gentiles,* I thought to myself, *but if I say Gentiles, he may say Jews.* Reminded of the prophet who said, "I have a word for someone in the room right now, and the Lord shows me that they are either a male or female," I said, "Both."

He said, "Wrong." Turning to Acts 9:15, he read to me the words spoken to Ananias as he reluctantly went to minister to the renowned persecutor, Saul of Tarsus: *"Go, for he is a chosen vessel of Mine to bear My name before Gentiles, kings, and the children of Israel."* He put his finger to my chest and uttered the unforgettable words: "Everyone forgets the kings!"

Who are the modern-day kings? They are the ones who occupy the high places, the spheres of influence in the seven mountains of culture. They write the songs you sing and make the movies you watch. They tell you what's in fashion and what's out. They design the iPhone and determine the price of gas. They craft the legislation you live with, and they send your sons to war. They straddle the thrones at the top of the seven mountains. Sociologists refer to them as remnant elites, but we might be more comfortable calling them gatekeepers. Simply stated, a mountain king is someone with a significant sphere of authority.

Every 7M (seven mountain) king has a position in a high place and influences their own sphere directly and other spheres indirectly. Kings do not have to be virtuous, but they do have to be competent or they won't last long because all kings know other kings who would like to take their thrones. This is not the culture of sheep; it is a culture more conducive to wolves. High places, the spheres of influence where kings position themselves, are the specific target and habitation of darkness. In fact, the apostle Paul revealed to the Ephesians that much of their wrestling was not with rulers made of flesh and blood, but rather against *"spiritual hosts of wickedness in the heavenly places"* (Eph. 6:12).

How does hell ensure control of this strategic ground? The fact that high-level spiritual powers guard these realms is indicated in the temptation of Jesus in the wilderness. Satan showed the prince of glory all the kingdoms of the world and said, *"All this authority I will give You, and their glory; for this has been delivered to me, and I give it to whomever I wish"* (Luke 4:6). Mountain kings wield incredible influence and power, and they need to hear the Gospel!

My Washington friend, having succeeded in besting me with the Pauline question, pointed out another verse to set me up for another question: "Look here, Lance, and notice where Jesus sent His disciples: *'Behold I send you out as sheep in the midst of wolves...'"* (Matt. 10:16). My friend then posed this question: "To whom are they to go when they visit the wolf pack?"

I was stumped again and came up with the rather lame spiritual answer, "Wherever God leads them?"

My mentor was not fazed at discovering my labyrinth of ignorance. He turned to another verse, *"Now whatever city or town you enter, inquire who in it is worthy, and stay there till you go out"* (Matt. 10:11).

No longer questioning me, he explained it this way:

At first I thought Jesus was telling the disciples to go to the nicest rabbi in town and start there, but really, that would be hard to do outside of Israel, and certainly it would be hard to imagine worthy rabbis who were also wolves. Who was Jesus telling them to start with? They were to go first to the community member whom the people placed the highest value upon, the one with worth and influence. The Gospel of the Kingdom is a proclamation to these wolf packs of influential 'mountain kings,' that another King has arrived and that this King is unlike any other. He is the judge of all men, the King over all kings. He is a good King and the best friend that any wolf has ever had.

In fact, if the wolf will cooperate, he will find that the One King who rules over all men and judges nations will help that wolf king succeed. This all-powerful One will drive out the influence of the powers of "spiritual wickedness," that fester and thrive off of the chaos and control they exercise in that king's domain. When wolf kings honor the King of glory, they do not become weak kings. Quite the contrary, they become truly great, and more so, they have authority to reveal the glory hidden within their sphere of authority.

Is there indeed glory in the seven mountains of culture? During the wilderness temptation of Jesus:

> *The devil, taking Him up on a high mountain, showed Him all the kingdoms of the world in a moment of time. And the devil said to Him, "All this authority I*

*will give You, and their glory; for this has been deliv-
ered to me, and I give it to whomever I wish"* (Luke
4:5-6).

The kingdoms of this world were not created by the devil. In
fact, he said, *"All this has been delivered to me, and I give it to whomever I wish."*

The kingdoms were made for humanity. These kingdoms possess
the capacity to reveal the glory of the One who called them into being.
In the last chapter of the Bible, when the will of God is fully manifest
on earth as it is in Heaven, there will be a complete takeover of the
earth. The kingdoms of this world will be the kingdoms of our Lord
and of His Christ, and the great city of God will be doing heavenly
business with kings of the earth: *"And they shall bring the glory and
the honor of the nations into it* [the celestial city]" (Rev. 21:26). Notice
how certain things continue on into eternity—an accessible heavenly
city and kings and nations on the earth! Especially notice that there is
an inexhaustible supply of "glory and honor" hidden under the sphere
of the kings in these nations.

DOES THE KINGDOM HAVE A CHURCH?

It seems clear that the Church has a Kingdom to proclaim, but
does the Kingdom have a church? This came home to me in a powerful way in the year 2000 when I was invited to South Korea to train
CEOs and executive coaches by my friend, Dr. Joseph Umidi, who was
at that time a professor at Regent University. I remember doing some
research before arriving, and finding out that 50 of the largest churches
in the world came out of South Korea. I thought that revealed something to me about the discipline and spirituality of the believers in the
culture, and therefore, I asked these businessmen the question: "How
many of the top 100 companies in the world are run by or owned by a

South Korean?" They were silent. I repeated the question through my interpreter twice because I thought they did not understand.

Then a man stood reluctantly to his feet and made a remarkable disclosure. "Sir," he said rather timidly, "I am neither a CEO nor an executive coach. I am here today because I needed to sneak in as a businessman to hear you. I pastor a youth church in Seoul, Korea, and the Lord told me the future of our ministry was tied into the revelation you will preach." He came up to the board where I had illustrated the seven mountains and pointed to the church mountain saying, "We have taught our people how to build the Church, but we have not taught them how to take the Kingdom!" as he circled the other six mountains.

Joseph wisely suggested that I be still and just watch what would happen next. Another young man stood up and said he had a confession to make. He was tall, had a deep voice, and spoke English rather well. He explained that he had attended Parker Business School in the United States and was a successful electronics entrepreneur; however, he had always felt a desire to be the president of South Korea. Up until that day, he was convinced that this was a selfish desire and that his best service was to contribute money to build the Church. But now he was publicly repenting of believing a lie. He realized that his political aspirations were not sinful after all.

The CEOs stood up next, but they did not rise to repent. They surrounded the young man in prayer and told him that, if he would do diligence and prepare himself as a qualified candidate, they would be honored to support his candidacy. It was a historic moment for me because I could see how quickly the Body of Christ can rise up with impact if the Kingdom is taught.

ALL THE MOUNTAINS BELONG IN THE KINGDOM

I think I was guilty at one time of doing the same thing to others that some well-meaning Christians did to that young man. When we think that the Church Mountain is the only spiritual mountain, we form a great divide between the Church and culture. We imply that the Church is the holy spiritual mountain and the rest of the mountains are of the world and profane.

The shocking truth is that each mountain is a spiritual mountain! The devil's skill in leading us to think differently has resulted in the spiritual invasion of foreign deities into every area once held by followers of Christ. As we surrendered our colleges and universities, the intellectual seducing spirits of false enlightenment took the hippies of the 1960s and made them the professors who teach your children in college today! This invasion is all the more ironic when you consider that the first 230 colleges and universities established in the United States were planted for the education and development of Christians, ministers in particular. This secular-sacred split has made the Church Mountain almost entirely irrelevant to society today.

The truth is that all nations are *already being discipled* through the belief systems of those occupying their high places, the peak institutions of a nation's mind molders. If the Church leaves a vacuum by failing to occupy these high places with the teaching of the Kingdom, the enemy will seek to disciple the nations by building strongholds of deception that are guarded and advanced through those decision makers who rise to the top of the seven mountains of culture.

Perhaps Jesus' description of the wheat and the tares makes more sense when seen in the light of our struggle in nations. The enemy had access to the harvest field to plant his corrupting seed *"while men slept"* (Matt. 13:25). The truth is that, as long as the Church thinks the purpose of the Great Commission is anything less than penetrating and occupying the mind molders of the nations in order to bring about a sustained influence that shapes the culture, we are asleep. The fields, our nations, are not only vulnerable to the enemy, but they are also being aggressively cultivated right under our noses.

In the Old Testament, God warned Israel that if they did not drive out the inhabitants of the land, the very peoples with whom they compromised would come after them. These inhabitants would be *"barbs in your eyes and thorns in your sides"* (Num. 33:55 NIV). The sober truth is that everywhere the Church is called to exercise her authority, but fails to, a vacuum opens for darkness to occupy. By rejecting the culture, we reject our spiritual authority to influence that culture. In the last days, however, there is no neutral territory. What we don't possess becomes fair game to occupy for the purpose of harassing us!

TAKING THE SEVEN MOUNTAINS

Here are some salient points to keep in mind as we embrace the message of the seven mountains.

The business of shifting culture or transforming nations does not require a majority of conversions. We make a mistake when we focus on winning a harvest in order to shape a culture. Together, Protestants and Catholics make up a 70 percent majority of the U.S. population, and as such already have a majority consensus on key matters affecting marriage and abortion. Yet they are still incapable of being more than a firewall to the minority, who are advancing a same-sex ideology. If we do not need more conversions to shift a culture, what do we need? We need more disciples in the right places, the high places. Minorities of people can shape the agenda, if properly aligned and deployed. The greatest gains in gay rights occurred during 10 years of our most conservative presidencies, and their movement has never been larger than 5 to 6 percent of the population.

The Church lacks cultural power because it focuses on changing the world from within the Church Mountain rather than releasing the Church into the marketplace to leaven all seven. The goal isn't to pull a convert out of the world and into a church, as we so often do.

The goal is to be the Church that raises up disciples who go into all the world. Taking the Gospel into all the world is no longer a journey simply of geography. The world is a matrix of overlapping systems or spheres of influence. We are called to go into the entire matrix and invade every system with an influence that liberates its fullest potential.

Isaiah described this process:

> *Now it shall come to pass in the latter days that the mountain of the Lord's house shall be established on the top of the mountains, and exalted above the hills; and all nations shall flow to it* (Isaiah 2:2).

The command of Jesus to teach and *"make disciples of nations"* (Matt. 28:19) implies that there is a distinctly biblical way of thinking and seeing the world. You do not need to know everything about every sphere, but you do need to master your own sphere by seeking out the wisdom of God—His way of thinking and seeing for that area. There is wisdom for every sphere, be it economics, art, marriage, education, government, and so forth. Start by mastering the fundamentals and trust that God will advance you to His hidden wisdom and revelation that, once applied, will produce superior results.

Each sphere has a unique structure, culture, and stronghold of thinking—a worldview of its own. The battle in each sphere is over the ideas that dominate that sphere and between the individuals who have the most power to advance those ideas. The apostle Paul addressed this battle in his admonition that we *"do not wrestle against flesh and blood, but against principalities, against powers..."* (Eph. 6:12). He tells us that, in dealing with these strongholds of thinking, our battle is in *"casting down arguments and everything that exalts itself against the knowledge of God"* (2 Cor. 10:5). The Church must be represented in each sphere if the power of darkness is to be broken. It is the Church alone that has spiritual authority to come against the gates of hell.

Those at the top of these spheres have the power to grant a person sphere authority by simply invitation. This is part of the power of letting your peace come upon people while staying in their house. When Saul permitted David to slip into the role of a soldier for a moment, David slew a giant and gained permanent access to the government mountain (see 1 Sam. 17). When Paul, a political prisoner, healed an island chief's father after a shipwreck, he was given an immediate upgrade of authority on the island (see Acts 28:7-10).

We carry something as kings and priests that is powerful. It is, in fact, a combined anointing. As kings, we have authority to administrate over earth and all demonic opposition. As priests, we have power to access heavenly places in Christ. Combined together, our identity as kings and priests allows us to access the throne of Grace and receive not only strength, but also instruction and divine blueprints that we then administrate on earth. We are salt. We slow down the decay of culture. We are also light, which means that we illuminate a pathway into a better future.

In fact, we who have tasted the powers of the age to come have authority to bring the power of that age into the present (see Heb. 6:5). As we do this, we access the power to manifest the testimony of Jesus. *"This gospel of the kingdom will be preached to all the nations as a* **witness,** *and then the end will come"* (Matt. 24:14). We are to be witnesses who demonstrate evidence of the reality of the Kingdom.

The world needs our witness of His Kingdom. When we witness to His Kingdom, we are manifesting the testimony of Jesus. Our witness shows that He is who He said He is and that He can do what He said He can do! "Worship God: *for the testimony of Jesus is the spirit of prophecy"* (see Rev. 19:10). To be light to the world is to reflect the illuminating power of the coming age right in the midst of this one.

It is to see the future and bring it into the present so that others can know what the coming Kingdom looks like.

What will being light to the world look like? What does it mean for us to bring the future to the present and thus display the Kingdom of God to the world? God is waiting for us to access His presence, His counsel, and His insight so that we can apply Heaven's solutions to earth and teach His ways by demonstrating solutions to problems. What Jesus demonstrated in healing human bodies is the same power that can transform nations. The leaves of the tree of life have power to heal nations! We have access to something that can fix *broken systems* among the nations. We have authority to heal sick systems in the seven mountains of culture. The following are the seven mountains and the maladies that humanity creates without someone to proclaim the truth and make crooked things straight:

1. **Religion:** People suffer from broken fellowship with God.

2. **Families:** Wounded fathers and mothers break from each other in divorce and their children, often unprotected, experience exploitation, abuse, and abandonment.

3. **Education:** Broken systems in the United States fail to educate students, and illiteracy causes over half of the world to miss out on the promise of prosperity.

4. **Government:** Broken systems of justice, destructive legislation, and corruption plague entire regions of the earth.

5. **Media and arts:** Broken oracles that do not speak the truth produce defiled images and destructive sounds and twist the image of what was made beautiful.

6. **Science and technology:** Broken remedies and perverted science wreak global destruction.

7. **Business:** Broken economies, robbed of opportunities and dignity, are full of greed and poverty.

These are the high places we have left for the devil to dominate because we have failed to see our role as healers and deliverers. This is why Jesus said, *"This gospel of the kingdom [not this Gospel of salvation] shall be preached in all the world for a **witness unto all nations"*** (Matt. 24:14). A witness does not guarantee the jury will decide in your favor, but it does mean that nations will be without excuse if they chose to follow another way. Those who are anti-Christ will be so because they reject the testimony of Jesus Christ.

Right now the only testimony we seem to be offering is through the Church Mountain as we proclaim the way of salvation and, perhaps, pray for a healing or word that endorses the supernatural authority of our message. Can you see how shallow our witness is when we refuse to make relevant the mighty power of Jesus over *all things?* We must not just limit His power to those things pertaining to the life to come.

THE HOLY NATION LIVING OUT THE KINGDOM

Dr. Henry Kissinger opens the first paragraph of his best-selling book on diplomacy in the most interesting language. In describing the flow of history, he leads into the emergence of the United States in its role over the last 100 years:

> Almost as if according to some natural law, in every century there seems to emerge a country with the power, the will, and the intellectual and moral impetus to shape the entire international system in accordance with its own values.[2]

A secular historian like Kissinger cannot see the invisible cosmic struggle of principalities and powers, working through demonized world rulers like Hitler, Stalin, or Mao. But he can see the aftermath in the formation of nations as the spoils of wars and upheavals. He is most certainly not trying to describe the role of the Church, but I think he defined a valid pattern in history that is setting things up for our role in this pivotal hour "as if according to some natural law, in every century there seems to emerge a country with the power.... the moral impetus to shape the entire international system." I believe that now we are that nation which seeks to emerge, the holy nation of Jesus-followers, the Church. We have been given heavenly authority and power in this final hour to impact the earth with our King's values—the message of His Kingdom.

The Church is one holy or set apart nation in the midst of a multitude of nations. The Reformers Pledge is for every nation. If what I am teaching is correct, all believers can become deliverers who arise like Joseph or Esther to save their nations and preserve the heritage of faith in their communities. You, more than any other person who does not know God, are uniquely called out from among others in your nation to be a citizen of Heaven with authority to bring Heaven and its unique resources and solutions into the earth. You can do this through the power of the Holy Spirit made manifest in your specific calling and assignment!

You are called to show forth the "praises" (the word here really can be interpreted as "the excellence") of Him who called you out of darkness (see 1 Pet. 2:9). You are called to enter into and engage in every earthly sphere of this world with a supernatural ability to manifest what God's Kingdom looks like. You are uniquely qualified to solve problems nobody else can solve! When you do so, you *"show forth the excellence of Him"* and build a platform of profound credibility from which you can teach others His ways.

We are entering a bigger battle than most of us appreciate. Something is emerging in the earth that seeks to rob nations of their ability to stand up in the freedom of their unique autonomy and reveal the glory God has deposited in them. God loves the idea of nations, and nations are designed to reveal His glory. They are His special interest. What does it look like when the will of God is done on earth as it is in Heaven? Look at Revelation 21:24-26 and you see it! The kings of the earth are ruling over nations! They exist in eternity. What do those kings do? They cultivate the potential in those nations to glorify God! *"They shall bring the glory and the honor of the nations"* into the city of God and display the beauty of what God has placed in the nations (Rev. 21:26). Jesus intends that you and I, as modern day kings and priests, teach nations His wonderful secrets. We are to make disciples, not of people only, but of nations.

None of this will be easy, which is why it is important to find your own company of like-minded believers whom you can stand with. If as believers, we fail to do this, we will surrender power to an increasingly hostile devil who knows that he has but a short time. Remembering that the Kingdom of Heaven suffers violence, it is important to note that we are engaged in a real war (see 2 Cor. 10:2-6). You are about to pioneer the last great chapter of the journey of the Church—into the Kingdom Age. It does not matter how large the obstacles are or how slender your present resources may appear to be. Jesus is once again telling His closest followers: *"Do not fear, little flock, for it is your Father's good pleasure to give you the kingdom!"* (Luke 12:32).

Chapter 9

STEWARDING FOR REFORMATION

C. PETER WAGNER

Pledge 9: I will be generous with my time, finances, gifts, and talents that God has entrusted to me to bring about public reformation of society (see Luke 19:11-26).

A major theme of this book is social reformation. Chapter after chapter reflects faith and hope that God's Kingdom will come here on earth as it is in Heaven. However, there seems to be a lurking, though unspoken, tinge of frustration. The question in the minds of many who are bold enough to probe beneath the surface is: Why haven't we seen more of the reformation that we've been talking about? In my personal reckoning, the season in which those of us who are charismatically inclined evangelicals began to put the Dominion Mandate front and center began in 1990, and it sharply accelerated after the turn of the century. We have been doing everything we know how to do to see our cities transformed. However, after 20 years we cannot point to a single city in America that has been reformed according to objective sociological measurements.

Yes, we have recorded and circulated encouraging anecdotes. There are many tangible signs that God is powerfully at work. Prayers have been answered, many of them dramatically. Prophecies have been fulfilled, some with extraordinary accuracy. Public officials have been converted and have dedicated their jurisdictions to God. Food supplies are reaching the hungry. Crime rates have dipped in a number of places. Proposition 8, defining marriage as a one-man, one-woman union, was victorious in the 2008 general election in California. New polls show that the majority of Americans are pro-life. We are praying harder than ever. We are worshiping more intensely. We have a record-breaking number of megachurches in the United States. And I could go on.

But the frustration persists. Reformation seems more elusive than we expected. Thoughtful people will naturally ask why. Are we doing something wrong? Is something missing? What changes do we need to make?

There are certainly many answers to these questions, and you will find some good ones throughout this book. But the particular missing piece that I want to address in this chapter is money. I repeat, *money*! Trust me. We will not see measureable, sustained transformation of our cities or states or nations if those who are providing strategic leadership do not have access to large sums of money. Throughout human history, three things have contributed toward the reformation of society more than anything else, namely, violence, knowledge, and wealth. And the greatest of these is wealth!

THE SPIRIT OF POVERTY

This has not been a very popular concept in the Religion Mountain. Many readers will be familiar with the 7M template, recently popularized by Lance Wallnau and discussed in the previous chapter. These seven chief mountains or molders of culture are contributors to the transformation of any society: Religion, Family, Government, Media, Education, Arts and Entertainment, and Business. Of all the seven mountains, the Religion Mountain typically has the most negative views of wealth. Why is this? I believe it is due largely to the pervasive influence that the spirit of poverty has been able to gain in the Religion Mountain.

Just a glance at Deuteronomy 28, for example, will quickly convince you that God's desire for His people is for them to prosper. The first half of Deuteronomy 28 lists the abundant blessings that God showers on those who obey Him, and the second half lists the curses that await those who disobey Him. Prosperity is the will of God, while poverty is the will of satan. The spirit of poverty is satan's agent assigned to infiltrate the Church with the pervasive notion that there is something very suspicious about prosperity. It made great strides in the Middle Ages when monks were required to take a vow of poverty. Since they were considered to be the most spiritual individuals in the community, the idea that poverty must be a sign of piety took root, and unfortunately, it persists throughout much of the Religion Mountain today.

I would go so far as to say that we will not experience sustained social reformation unless and until we successfully bind the spirit of poverty through the blood of Jesus Christ and command it to loose its hold on the people of God. I believe that we need to come against this spirit of darkness by moving in the opposite spirit, which is the spirit of prosperity. It is wrong and even selfish to expect God to provide only "sufficiency" because mere sufficiency does not allow you to supply funding for God's causes—you need to spend all you have on yourself. No, believers should learn how to enjoy prosperity without succumbing to greed or covetousness or above all to mammon, an equally pernicious agent of darkness. Godly prosperity, then, will provide surplus wealth available for advancing the Kingdom of God.

THE DOMINION MANDATE

Let's think about advancing the Kingdom of God. Jesus taught us to pray, *"Your kingdom come. Your will be done on earth as it is in heaven"* (Matt. 6:10). All we need to do is go back to Genesis chapter 1 to be reminded of God's original purpose for creation. After creating everything else in five days, He created humans on the sixth. He told them to be fruitful and multiply and fill the earth, and then He informed them that they were supposed to take dominion over what He had just created (see Gen. 1:28). Although this was God's plan, it was hijacked by satan's success in tempting Adam and Eve to disobey God. The result was that satan usurped the authority that Adam was supposed to have over the creation and went on to become the god of this age and the prince of the power of the air (see Eph. 6:12).

Satan virtually had his way over the human race until Jesus came. Jesus was called the "last Adam" because, through His death and resurrection, He was to turn things back around (see 1 Cor. 15:20-28,45). He came to seek and to save that which was lost. What was lost? The dominion over creation was lost because Adam forfeited it in the Garden of Eden. Jesus brought a new Kingdom, the Kingdom of God, which was to replace the perverse kingdom that satan had established. He came to reconcile the world back to Himself, and He assigned the ministry of reconciliation to us (see 2 Cor. 5:18). Since then, it has been the responsibility of the people of God, empowered by the Holy Spirit, to regain the dominion that Adam was originally supposed to have. This is the Dominion Mandate.

Take, for instance, Jesus' Great Commission: *"Go therefore and make disciples of all the nations..."* (Matt. 28:19). Previously many of us interpreted that to mean that we were to go into the nations in order to win as many souls as possible. Now, in light of the Dominion Mandate, we take it literally and see that we are to disciple *nations* as whole social units. Our task, then, is nothing less than reforming nations or people groups or social units of whatever scope. The values and blessings of God's Kingdom must become characteristic of whole cities or states or countries. But practically speaking, part of the process of making that happen is to have large amounts of wealth available.

By way of example, many of us who are advocating social change are fond of pointing out that it does not necessarily require a majority to bring it about. A favorite, albeit tragic, illustration relates to the gay agenda in the U.S. Even though the homosexual population of our nation numbers is very small as a percentage, a concerted effort on their part has succeeded in altering the social psychology of our country. Homosexuality is now gaining the status of an acceptable form of sexual orientation, and state after state is legitimizing gay marriage. How can such a fractional minority accomplish such a lofty goal? Obviously it is because their leadership was able to forge a brilliant strategy designed to penetrate all seven mountains. But the strategy itself in all likelihood would not have succeeded were it not for massive funding. I subscribe to *The Chronicle of Philanthropy*, and I stand amazed (as well as appalled!) at the huge quantity of grant money directed to gay causes across our nation!

It is no wonder that Solomon said, *"...Money answers everything"* (Eccl. 10:19). In light of this, we must take the steps necessary to see that wealth pours into the hands of Kingdom-minded and Kingdom-motivated leaders who can successfully move God's people into sustained reformation of society. This is the will of God. The Bible says, *"Your gates shall be open continually; they shall not be shut day or night, that men may bring you the wealth of the Gentiles..."* (Isa. 60:11).

THE GREAT TRANSFER
OF WEALTH

A great transfer of wealth from the unrighteous to the righteous is imminent. The assurance of this has come through a number of recognized prophets who are hearing from the Holy Spirit. I have learned to listen carefully to the prophets because the Bible says, *"Surely the Lord God does nothing, unless He reveals His secret to His servants the prophets"* (Amos 3:7). These prophecies began in the early 1990s, and they have continued. There have been a few promising signs, such as donations of $1.5 billion to the Salvation Army and $50 million to Wycliffe Bible Translators and $30 million to Young Life. But much more is to come. Why has it been delayed for almost 20 years?

The answer to this must have to do with God's timing. The wealth undoubtedly is there, but apparently we are not yet ready to receive it. For one thing, I believe that God was waiting for the biblical government of the Church to come into place under apostles and prophets. But this happened in 2001 when, at least according to my estimates, the Second Apostolic Age began. What more? I now think that in order for us to be able to handle the wealth responsibly, we need to recognize, identify, affirm, and encourage the ministry of apostles in the six non-Religion mountains. They may or may not want to use the term "apostle," but they will function in Kingdom-based leadership roles characterized by supernaturally empowered wisdom and authority. We have more work to do here.

INFRASTRUCTURE DESIGN

Meanwhile, God has given us a design for an infrastructure that can handle any quantity of Kingdom wealth responsibly. It begins with the four links in the chain of wealth transfer:

THE FOUR LINKS

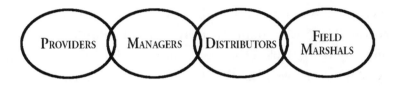

As you can see, the links are Providers, Managers, Distributors, and Field Marshals. The Field Marshals are already deployed to the front lines of expanding God's Kingdom. They are called and committed to preaching and activating the Gospel of the Kingdom. They are constantly healing the sick, casting out devils, preaching God's salvation to hungry souls, multiplying churches, caring for the poor, and transforming society. Most of them are doing an outstanding job, but virtually all have a ceiling that keeps them from doing all that they are capable of, and that ceiling is almost always *money*! It is the responsibility of the other three links in the chain to see that this ceiling is removed.

The first link, the Providers, must already be in place as well. I don't think that God would have given us the word that funds will be released unless the wealth was actually there, and that would obviously be in the hands of the Providers. Undoubtedly, more Providers will be added, and many existing Providers will generate much more wealth, but the initial amount must currently be in place.

I am personally most interested in the Distributors link because that is where I feel I have a role. There are two kinds of distributors, Narrow-Band Distributors and Wide-Band Distributors. If the link was divided in two, the Narrow-Band Distributors would be toward the right, in direct contact with the Field Marshals. Using examples from some contributors to this book, Ché Ahn, John Arnott, Bill Johnson, and Heidi Baker would be Narrow-Band Distributors because they each oversee networks of Field Marshals. When Ché Ahn receives funds, for instance, he will not distribute those funds to the American Bible Society or the Southern Baptist International Mission Board or Wycliffe Bible Translators, worthy as those ministries may be. Ché is responsible under God for his own apostolic sphere that is represented by Harvest International Ministry. His Kingdom-oriented apostolic infrastructure is poised to make good use of huge amounts of wealth for God's causes.

Wide-Band Distributors would be toward the left side of the Distributor link, in direct touch with the Managers link on one hand, and with the Narrow-Band Distributors on the other. This is where I would locate myself. I do not have a network of Field Marshals, but I am networked with hundreds of active apostles, a good many of whom are Narrow-Band Distributors overseeing Field Marshals in virtually every part of the world. My role in distributing the wealth that is being transferred will be to get it into the hands of Kingdom-minded apostles who will know exactly what to do with it.

I now have established the necessary infrastructure to implement this Wide-Band Distribution in a responsible way with organizations such as the Global Distribution Network and The Hamilton Group, named in honor of Alexander Hamilton, who was my four-times great grandfather. Hamilton, as you may recall, was our first secretary of the Treasury, and he laid the foundation for the American financial system as we have known it through the years. We want our Kingdom distribution structure to reflect the creativity and the integrity of its namesake.

MINISTRY REVENUE FUNDS

I now want to address the second link in the chain, that is, Managers. At the moment, this is our weakest link, and I wouldn't be surprised if God might be delaying the great transfer of wealth until we strengthen this link. The general idea is that wealth that originates with the Providers is multiplied by the Managers before it goes further down the chain. For example if a Provider releases $100,000, it would be nice if it were $300,000 by the time it got to the Distributors. The multiplication difference would be due to the Managers.

My vision is that we begin to shift our ministries and international apostolic networks from our current donor-based funding to revenue-based funding. In our traditional procedure, Narrow-Band Distributors—let's call them ministry leaders—have relied on donations from Providers to sustain their ministries. They have mailing lists. They assign staff members to "donor development." They know Providers who are attracted to their ministry and who will respond to appeals for cash flow or special projects. They spend their money well and thereby maintain the trust of the Providers. When a new need arises, they go back to the Providers, some of whom function like ministry ATMs. This donor-based system of funding has worked fairly well in the past, but I personally sense a change coming. I am in direct touch with several ministries that are finding that donor-based funding is not as productive as it once was.

A substantial step forward would be for ministries and apostolic networks to establish ministry revenue funds that would bring the Manager link more directly into the picture. In other words, a Provider would not only donate to a ministry's cash flow or special projects, all of which would be spent as expected, but would also contribute principal to a fund that would not be spent, but managed. The proceeds from this revenue fund would then be available for cash flow or projects. Ideally the revenue fund would become large enough to provide the income needed to cover the annual administrative costs of the ministry initially and then be available for projects and expansion. Many will recognize that universities and other institutions have functioned this way with endowment funds for a long time. I personally feel that it is better to avoid the traditional term *endowment* for our Kingdom purposes because of some baggage that may come with it. "Ministry revenue fund" will work.

MANAGING MONEY IS BIBLICAL

In order for ministry revenue funds to accomplish their purpose, they must not only be managed, but they must be *successfully* managed. That means that we should shoot for a rate of return that is well above what has been considered as normal in the industry.

I have spent a good bit of time revisiting Jesus' well-known parables in Matthew 25 and Luke 19 dealing with talents and minas. First, we need to get rid of the common allegorical interpretation that in these parables Jesus is instructing us to use our personal gifts and abilities and talents in such a way that will please Him. No. These parables are dealing with finances and financial markets. The talent was a monetary instrument worth around $1 million and the mina one worth around $10,000. In each parable, the workers were instructed by the CEO to *trade* the money entrusted to them. In Luke 19:15 we are specifically told that the earnings came from "trading," the Greek for which is *diapragmateuomai*, a technical term from the financial industry of the day. Notice that the returns did not come from the restaurant business or from real estate or from imports/exports or from manufacturing, but from managing money. This directly relates to the second link of the chain of wealth transfer.

We do not know what kind of financial trading they did, but a reasonable case can be made that it could have been a foreign currency exchange. In any case, the returns were considerably above what we consider normal in the industry. In Matthew they were 100 percent, and in Luke 500 percent and 1000 percent. Over what period of time did this return occur? Over the time it took for the CEO to take a trip and return. Since few trips take as much as a year, it could well be that they were annual rates of return or better. I am not sure we could expect rates of return near these for our ministry revenue funds today, but let's keep in mind that they are biblical!

Let me summarize what I have just said. If we are going to generate the massive financing required for reformation of society, we will need all four links of the chain of wealth transfer in action, and the weakest one at this writing is that of Managers. This is the time for Kingdom-minded financial managers to step up to the plate and move the whole Kingdom of God forward. They will be functioning as apostles or equivalent leaders in the Business Mountain, and their ministry will be just as important for the Kingdom as pastoring a church or going to the mission field or traveling as an evangelist. Did you notice that I used the word *ministry*? I am convinced that true biblical ministry happens in the workplace through those who are making money for the Kingdom just as much as it does through those who are, for example, writing spiritual songs and leading congregations in worship.

MECHANISMS FOR WEALTH TRANSFER

There are three ways that we can expect to see wealth transferred into the Kingdom of God. It is important to observe the big picture so as not to fall into the trap of highlighting just one of these mechanisms, as though it were the only way that God would choose to work.

- **Supernatural transfer:** God arranges circumstances so that wealth is entrusted to Distributors or Field Marshals without any overt action on their part. A biblical example of this is the Israelites leaving Egypt. When they got to the desert they were prosperous, and they didn't get their money from making bricks without straw. God had moved supernaturally in the hearts of the idol-worshiping Egyptians to turn huge amounts of wealth over to God's people. In our day, the $1.5 billion gift from Joan Kroc to the Salvation Army was not generated from ringing bells over kettles at Christmas time, but it was a supernatural transfer.

- **Power to get wealth:** Deuteronomy 8:18 says, *"You shall remember the Lord your God, for it is He who gives you **power to get wealth**, that He may establish His covenant...."* Here the responsibility for gaining wealth falls on the individual to whom God gives supernatural power for extraordinary increase. One way of paraphrasing this Scripture is to hear God saying: "I'm assigning you the responsibility to be prosperous so that you can fund My Kingdom." The more Kingdom-minded believers who become wealthy, the faster God's Kingdom will expand.

- **A Combination of the two:** Going back to the Israelites leaving Egypt, the supernatural transfer of wealth was accomplished by a seldom-recognized factor: the women! Exodus 3:22 says,

"But every woman shall ask of her neighbor... articles of silver, articles of gold...So shall you plunder the Egyptians." God gave the women extraordinary power to get wealth from their Egyptian neighbors, and apparently it wouldn't have happened without them. Even today, some large amounts of supernatural funding will be available only if we see ourselves as being assigned fiscal responsibility and if we determine to take the proper steps to secure the funding, even when it may come from unusual sources or through unusual means.

THE HAMILTON GROUP

Keeping in mind what I have just said, I have recently joined with some friends and formed an organization that is poised to receive and distribute whatever quantities of wealth God desires to release. When I described the Distributors link in the chain of wealth transfer a while ago, I mentioned The Hamilton Group (THG), named after my ancestor, Alexander Hamilton. My vision statement for THG is "Sophisticated Philanthropy for Apostolic Distribution." The first part, *sophisticated philanthropy,* a term I am borrowing from Bruce Cook,[1] means philanthropy specifically directed toward worthwhile goals, in this case extending God's Kingdom. Amazingly, some philanthropists evaluate their success only on how much they give, not on how much good their money might or might not be doing. THG, to the contrary, strictly monitors and audits whatever grants it makes.

The second part, *for apostolic distribution,* means that those who oversee and prioritize those Field Marshals who would qualify to receive funding are themselves recognized and experienced apostles. They understand the Dominion Mandate, and they have efficient international administrative structures in place to use Kingdom funding responsibly. Some philanthropic agencies operate from a "seeker" mode. They seek funds through fund-raising departments, and they seek projects through research departments. Conversely, THG operates from a "server" mode. It serves Providers who desire a trustworthy infrastructure to distribute their Kingdom funds, and it serves the apostles who already have Kingdom-advancing projects in place all over the world and who will responsibly monitor their progress.

RECEIVING KINGDOM PROSPERITY

I believe that each one of us should desire prosperity, should pray for prosperity, and should expect that God will prosper us. Why? What does my prosperity have to do with the Kingdom of God? The answer is quite simple. If you're Kingdom-minded, you are tuned in to philanthropy because the root meaning of *philanthropy* is "loving people." You want to help other people as much as you can. But you cannot help others with what you do not have. If you are struggling through life with mere sufficiency, you must use all you have for personal survival. However, the richer you are, the more you can provide for the Kingdom.

I like author Frank Damazio's plea that we all seek to be "surplus people." He says:

> Surplus living is a biblical concept taught by Christ and the apostles. Surplus is a kingdom principle... Surplus is more than is required or needed—over and above the norm. Surplus spills over the top. It is more than sufficient. It is excessive, beyond what you have expected.[2]

He then goes on to say,

Prosperity begins with your decision to believe that God desires to use you to bless others and that to do so means you must have more than enough—you must have an overflow, a surplus, an abundance.[3]

Satan will do all he can to block such thinking from your mind and from your spirit. Satan is the author of poverty, and he will send the spirit of poverty that I mentioned earlier to keep you from receiving all that God has for you. He will even try to make you think that Jesus was poor, which is far from reality. Poverty is not a sign of spirituality or Christ-likeness. Instead of being oppressed by the spirit of poverty, move in the opposite spirit, which is the spirit of prosperity. Freedom in Christ means freedom to receive the abundance that God has reserved for you.

FOUR STEPS TOWARD GODLY PROSPERITY

Those who agree with what I have just said will be asking, "What steps do I need to take to, as rapidly as possible, become a surplus person who can help finance the advance of the Kingdom of God?" First, pray hard and ask God for a practical answer to the question that is tailor-made to your particular position in life. You are one of a kind. As you do this, simultaneously follow these four steps as much as you possibly can:

1. **Listen to the prophets.** Identify some who are respected and experienced prophets in the Body of Christ. Get as near to them as you can. If possible, become personal friends with them. Be on the alert for guidance that God may give to you through them. The Bible says, *"...Believe in the Lord your God and you shall*

be established; believe His prophets and you shall ***prosper***" (2 Chron. 20:20). As I have discovered in my own personal life, prophets often hold the keys to prosperity for us.

2. **Delight in the law of the Lord.** Delighting in God's law means that you deeply desire to please Him and obey Him in all things. God's Word provides the compass for every phase of your life. Some refer to this as recognizing the Lordship of Christ. Psalm 1 begins by saying that the person who delights in the law of the Lord is *"like a tree planted by the rivers of water"* and *"whatever he does shall **prosper**"* (Ps. 1:3). If you walk closely with God, He will make you a surplus person.

3. **Confess all known sins.** Look at what the Bible says: *"He who covers his sins will **not prosper**, but whoever confesses and forsakes them will have mercy"* (Prov. 28:13). This warning brings up a possible blockage to the abundance that God desires to pour out. Do a spiritual inventory and be honest with yourself. Is there anything in the past that you haven't dealt with? Or even worse, do you have "issues" in the present that you keep sweeping under the rug? If so, now is the time to confess them and forsake them. It will open the door to prosperity.

4. **Follow John Wesley's advice.** Here is one of the most famous quotes from John Wesley. It is

so clear that it needs no explanation. If you do what Wesley says, you can expect God to help you become a surplus person who has resources for advancing the Kingdom of God:

- Earn all you can.

- Save all you can.

- Give all you can.[4]

OPEN THE GATES BY GIVING

Wesley's third admonition was "Give all you can." Let's look more closely at that for a moment. Earlier I mentioned Isaiah 60 where it says, *"Your gates shall be open continually."* If you want God to open the gates of prosperity in your life, you must be a giving person, and you must give cheerfully. Think hard about this word from the Lord: *"There is one who scatters, yet increases more; and there is one who withholds more than is right, but it leads to poverty. The generous soul will be made rich..."* (Prov. 11:24-25). Why wouldn't God want you rich? He for sure doesn't want you poor. He doesn't want you to just scrape by with bare sufficiency for your own needs. The richer you are, the more you can do your part to finance the advance of the Kingdom and the reformation of society.

But in order to get there, you must follow God's rules for giving. I acknowledge that there are different interpretations of the biblical material on giving, but I have personally come to the conclusion that if you are going to be a reformer you must give tithes, offerings, and firstfruits.

Tithes are clearly mandated by Scripture. My advice is to take Malachi 3 seriously as a word from God and not try to argue it away. It tells you that if you don't bring your tithes (10 percent of your income) to God's storehouse, you are robbing God! But if you do tithe, God will open the windows of Heaven and pour out blessing. I shy away from legalism, but I interpret the tithe literally, and I strictly and consistently practice it in my own life.

Offerings are what you give over and above your tithe. They are also mentioned in Malachi 3:8. Tithes are not *your* money; you are giving God back *His* 10 percent. Offerings, then, are your own money that you are giving to God and His Kingdom. Be generous with offerings over and above your tithe.

Firstfruits represent a special kind of giving over and beyond tithes and offerings. Numbers 18 contrasts firstfruits and tithes. Tithes were for the Levites, and firstfruits were for the priests. In modern language, tithes are for the pastors or the storehouse, and firstfruits are for the apostles. Firstfruits, the first and the best, are given by faith at the beginning of the harvest, and tithes are returned to God after the harvest. Do you want to prosper? *"Honor the Lord with your possessions, and with the **firstfruits** of all your increase; so your barns will be filled with plenty, and your vats will overflow with new wine"* (Prov. 3:9-10).

KINGDOM-MINDED REFORMERS

It will take money to finance the reformation. God wants this money in the hands of Kingdom-minded reformers. Do you want to be part of that company? If any of us says yes to that question, here is a checklist of our required characteristics:

- We obey the Lord. We are sons and daughters of our heavenly Father, and our deepest desire is to do His will. Our lives will be holy, free from blemish, reproach, or blame.

- We step out in faith. We believe and do not doubt. Skepticism will not creep in. Worry and fear have no place in our minds or in our hearts.

- We give extravagantly. *"He who sows sparingly will reap sparingly, and he who sows bountifully will reap bountifully"* (2 Cor. 9:6).

- We humble ourselves. We acknowledge that all that we are and all that we possess are by God's grace. We refuse to become self-reliant and say, *"My power and the might of my hand have gained me this wealth"* (Deut. 8:17).

- We keep the true goal in sight. We focus on the Kingdom of God. *"Your kingdom come. Your will be done on earth as it is in heaven"* (Matt. 6:10).

Chapter 10

ALIGNING FOR REFORMATION

CHUCK PIERCE

Pledge 10: I will love God's Church, walk in unity
with God's people, and be in proper alignment and
covering with those who are in spiritual authority
in my life, beside me in serving the Lord, and
entrusted to me for oversight. I will pursue
unity, alignment, and righteousness within these
relationships, knowing that it takes this cohesion in
the Body of Christ to reform society (see Ps. 133).

ALIGNMENT HEALS AND REFORMS

The last two decades of my life, I have walked with Dr. C. Peter
Wagner. Peter and Doris Wagner are known in Christendom as para-
digm changers. Peter is a missiologist who served in the School of

World Mission at Fuller Theological Seminary in Pasadena. Both he and Doris were missionaries in Bolivia.

In the 1980s, Peter met another man, John Wimber, and together they were used to develop a shift in the Church world regarding signs, wonders, and miracles. Peter is known for his work in the area of communicating an understanding of spiritual warfare during the 1990s. He wrote a series of books on warfare prayer that are now classics for the Body of Christ to use for generations to come. As we entered the new millennium, he was a leader in the restoration of the apostle gift in the Kingdom of God and mobilized apostles throughout the world. Now he is spearheading a movement to see transformation in the earth realm.

I have been honored to walk with him since the beginning of the 1990s. We have attempted to model how a prophet and apostle align to accomplish the will of God in the earth in our generation. Throughout this chapter, I will relate what we have learned about the power of spiritual alignment and submission.

We have moved from a Church Age to expressing God's Kingdom Dominion in the earth. The Kingdom of God represents God's rule in the earth realm. The King is moving us from *just going to church* to *understanding His Kingdom in our territory*. He is bringing us into a place of dominion, occupation, and ruling with Him in the spheres and places He has assigned to us. Peter Wagner calls this shift in the earth "The Third Great Reformation." I believe that the key to this season of reformation is spiritual alignment.

Another person whom I have aligned with through the years is Dutch Sheets. Dutch is known for his book on intercessory prayer.[1] He is a passionate spiritual leader who has fire in his bones. His heart is to see a nation change. He is a reformer. I use both Dutch and Peter as examples of how gifts of the Spirit are aligning and synergizing. When we align, we gain a greater strength to accomplish God's plan in the earth. You will read more in this chapter about our alignment as we visited all 50 states.

Jesus sent His disciples by twos to accomplish the harvest. Dutch has the best explanation of alignment of anyone I know. He uses a Greek word found in the New Testament, *katartizo,* which means "to adjust; to put a thing in its appropriate position."[2] The word is used in context with mending nets (see Matt. 4:21), repairing schisms or relational breaks (see 1 Cor. 1:10), and even restoring broken lives (see Gal. 6:1). The word has also been used to describe the restoration of a dislocated joint or a broken bone.

So as you can see, the concept of this word involves proper alignment, including realignment, resulting in healing or restoration. Dutch Sheets calls God "the holy Chiropractor." He says this, "God adjusts us also. He has adjusted me many times—my heart, my thinking, my direction, even my hopes and dreams. He also adjusts nations."[3] In *Releasing the Prophetic Destiny of a Nation,* Dutch also shares this:

> God uses that word to describe the proper alignment of the seasons of time. In other words, He declares in advance His plans for the future of nations and peoples of the earth. Hebrews 11:3 says, in its more literal and accurate rendering, that the "ages" (Greek—*aiones*) were "properly aligned or connected" (Greek—*katartizo*) by the word or decree of the Lord. In other words, God decreed the flow of history.
>
> At times, however, breaches occur that cause the need for corrections in this flow of history. Simply stated, history needs to be healed. Whether it is on a corporate level, such as the Fall of humanity, wars, racial division, etc., or on a more individual level in the sense of broken relationships, loss, etc., the fact is that history often needs healing. This corporate level of healing is

what is referred to in verses like Isaiah 58:12: *"Those from among you will rebuild the ancient ruins; you will raise up the age-old foundations; and you will be called the repairer of the breach, the restorer of the streets in which to dwell"* (NASB). (See also Isaiah 61:4.) This is also the concept spoken of in Second Chronicles 7:14: "[If] *My people who are called by My name humble themselves and pray and seek My face and turn from their wicked ways, then I will hear from heaven, will forgive their sin and will heal their land"* (NASB).

God, the holy Chiropractor of history, heals our dislocations—our subluxations. He "katartisis-es the aiones." This occurs through repentance, reconciliation, forgiveness, prayer, fasting, prophetic decrees, and other biblical actions, all of which are effective because of the blood of His Son, Jesus Christ.[4]

AN AWAKENING TO THE NEED FOR FATHERS

When I was 16, my Dad died tragically. Three months before that, my grandfather on my mother's side had died. After my Dad's death, his father, my paternal grandfather, made a choice not to see us again because of the pain of our family loss and all the encompassing circumstances related to this trauma.

Immediately, there was a major gap in my life; there was no paternal authority structure. I had experienced the Lord and seen Him move many times, but I must confess, I took advantage of no male authority in my life...until one day. My mother instructed me not to allow an acquaintance of mine to drive my car. I disregarded her request. Later that day when I was with my boss and we were on assignment, we came through the center of town and saw my vehicle in an accident.

My boss, who was not a devoted Christian, spoke to me and said, "Someone upstairs is trying to get your attention and reorder your life." Then the Lord spoke to me and said, "I have already chosen the fathers for your life for the future. Submit to them when I bring them into your path, and you will prosper!"

This statement changed my thinking, my actions, and my life. Since that day, I have been in a lifelong learning course on apostolic alignment. I did not understand the concept of apostolic alignment, but I did understand the power of submission to those who were divinely positioned in my life: bosses, professors, doctors, pastors, mission executives, and apostolic ministry leaders. Because I have been willing to submit and align with the leaders and then work with the teams that God placed in my life, I have prospered. I will discuss apostolic teams later in the chapter.

THE FAITH FROM OUR SPIRITUAL MOTHERS

I love the way Paul wrote to his spiritual son, Timothy. In his writing as a spiritual father, he acknowledged the mothers (natural and spiritual) that Timothy had to produce the faith that dwelled richly in him. Not only was I privileged to have a godly mother and grandmother, but I have had several spiritual mothers who have taught me the Word of the Lord and kept me moving in holiness and faith. In Second Timothy 1:3-7, Paul wrote:

> *I thank God, whom I serve with a clear conscience the way my forefathers did, as I constantly remember you in my prayers night and day, longing to see you, even as I recall your tears, so that I may be filled with joy. For I am mindful of the sincere faith within you, which first dwelt in your grandmother Lois and your mother Eunice, and I am sure that it is in you as well. For this*

reason I remind you to kindle afresh the gift of God
which is in you through the laying on of my hands. For
God has not given us a spirit of timidity, but of power
and love and discipline (2 Timothy 1:3-7 NASB).

To be properly aligned, you need to adhere to both spiritual fathers and mothers. I always say, "You need fathers and mothers to protect you from dysfunctional patterns of behavior in your family. And the family is the first war unit that was created on earth."

GOD HAS AN ORDER

We need our mothers and fathers to be in our lives in order to live a life of faith. However, *alignment* has to do with us maturing and coming to the unity of the faith. This includes us always remaining part of the Body. We were never meant to be independent, but *dependent* on one another. Ephesians 4 is about alignment, unity, faith, and maturing. We will discuss this more fully later in this chapter. Without proper alignment and discipleship, we do not see the necessary order to overcome and triumph in our life situations and the mission calls that are extended from Heaven from generation to generation.

God has an order of alignment in His government. A good house has to have an aligned foundation. A great house must have an order. Order is a military and mathematical term. In First Corinthians 12:28-30, we find God's order:

And God has appointed in the church, first apostles,
second prophets, third teachers, then miracles, then
gifts of healings, helps, administrations, various kinds
of tongues. All are not apostles, are they? All are not
prophets, are they? All are not teachers, are they? All are

not workers of miracles, are they? All do not have gifts of healings, do they? All do not speak with tongues, do they? All do not interpret, do they? But earnestly desire the greater gifts... (1 Corinthians 12:28-30 NASB).

Therefore if we are aligned and ordered properly, we create the full display of God's glory in the earth. This reforms the earth and culture around us.

We find that God has a perfect order in His Kingdom to break defilement and bring prophetic fulfillment. When Jesus was ascending into Heaven, Ephesians 4:8 says that He gave gifts to humankind. In First Corinthians 12, Paul shows how each member of the Body of Christ has an individual relationship with the Lord, but is also corporately dependent upon every other member in the Body. When the Lord knit each one of us together in the womb, He built a plan of action into our spirits. Not only does He know who we are, He knows what we should be and do individually and corporately to accomplish His plan in our generation. In other words, we can't fully come into our prophetic destiny unless we align our gift properly with other members of the Body.

For us to see God's order, apostles must be first and prophets second; then we can pastor and teach the sheep properly. This movement is much more than people finding Christ and needing each other. This is a movement with new order and authority. This is a movement that will see the world evangelized. We have begun to see a shift from scattered sheep to the Triumphant Reserve; His family is being restored and becoming a viable, holy army in the earth! The works of Jesus are being done again, and with the technological ability to communicate around the world, I believe we are seeing the "greater works" Christ said we would do. Each gift in the Body of Christ that is resident in all who believe in the Lord Jesus Christ must come into the fullness of its God-designed destiny!

To accomplish this requires that all the ascension gifts are aligned: *apostles, prophets, evangelists, pastors, and teachers* (see Eph. 4:11). A plan of dominion for "this age" has been released, and the Kingdom of God is moving forward!

God's Unfolding Battle Plan is a book that reveals what is ahead for the Body of Christ over the next several years. In this book I share:

> Governments of the world cannot fully change until the government of God here on earth aligns itself and represents the order of God. That means leaders in the Church must get their act together! I see many denominations or wineskins of the past fading and becoming irrelevant by 2016. There have already been many changes. We have become aware of God's foundational plan of apostles, prophets, evangelists, pastors and teachers. We are learning how to interact with each other. We are letting go of old methods of operation and embracing new ways of worship.
>
> The real war in days ahead will come over how we fellowship. We will have to learn how to operate in decentralized fellowship. In other words, we won't all be going to church every Sunday. That form of worship is changing rapidly. At the same time, corporate worship gatherings in certain territories will break through into new levels of revelation. I am not talking about extra-biblical revelation—the Bible has been canonized; it is the established Word of God. However, I believe there is revelation coming that will cause the Word to become even more applicable for this age, while also giving us strategies to defeat the enemy. Many

of what are now corporate warfare worship gatherings will turn into times of travail, and the result will be changed nations. As we come together and worship in such settings, we will gain new strategies for how to govern in our spheres of authority.[5]

WARRING IN A KINGDOM THAT IS ALIGNED

These are wonderful but dangerous times. The Body of Christ is maturing, but it's not yet mature. Perhaps more than at any other time in history, the Church is in a crisis of competition for harvest with other organized religious forces, including Islam, Buddhism, Hinduism, and a host of other "-isms." Confrontations with demonic forces behind opposing belief systems will be the norm for the future, and God is calling His Body to prepare for the warfare we are entering even now. Part of our preparation is to develop an understanding of our role in the future establishment of governments. Both the Body of Christ and the governments of nations are already changing drastically. Through these changes, however, our most important understanding is how we are aligned in Kingdom government.

God's Kingdom rule is different. The Kingdom is *good news*! In the Kingdom, Christ accomplishes His mediational authority. He rules in the earth realm *through* His heavenly Kingdom, with His subjects responding to Him from both an individual and a collective identity. In other words, we respond to Him as both a single citizen of His Kingdom and through our union as the corporate Body. This is essential to understand if we are going to affect a territory. Man-made kingdoms have a king who has ultimate and solo authority over the rule of his kingdom. But in the Lord's divine plan, we as His subjects have been given Kingdom power. We can enter and rule *with* Him. Let's look at this unique spiritually aligned rule in God's Kingdom.

In Ephesians 2:20, the foundation of this Kingdom government is once again mentioned as *"having been built on the foundation of the apostles and prophets, Jesus Christ Himself being the chief cornerstone"* (NASB). The Kingdom is made up of people who have submitted themselves to be ruled by God. His Kingdom is *not* made up of law, but is governed by grace. His Kingdom has an administration. There are ways that He "does ministry" in His Kingdom. Every kingdom has a culture, and God's Kingdom has its own very unique culture. I believe this is the most difficult concept for us to understand. Many times we become a part of God's Kingdom, yet we continue to operate in the culture of this world. That is the wrong approach!

Although He has ways to take care of all the needs in His Kingdom, the Lord's Kingdom is not based just on needs, nor is it based on worldly patterns. When King David deviated from the Lord's pattern, he found himself in trouble or creating trouble. It was the same way with Moses; when he struck the rock the second time, instead of speaking to it, he deviated from the pattern of Heaven. This caused him to lose the right to enter into the promise that he was pressing and leading the people toward (see Num. 20:1-13). We can never forget that God's Kingdom cannot be comprehended by the natural mind. Our minds are in transition until they are fully overcome by the Spirit of grace. Until then, our carnal minds remain in enmity with God (see Rom. 8:5-8).

One final thought on God's Kingdom: It cannot be obtained by ambition. That is what Judas had to learn. Judas never aligned! It is easy to point the condescending finger at Judas, but we must remember that John and James, the Sons of Thunder, had to learn the same lesson. When they aspired to use divine authority to pronounce destructive judgment, Jesus said to them, *"You do not know what manner of spirit you are of"* (Luke 9:55). The Kingdom cannot be postponed. It is here and now within those who have submitted to the

King. It is filled with glory. And it is God's intent for the ambassadors of that Kingdom to carry His glory throughout the world until the whole world has experienced true transformation, the kind that brings *real* life and freedom to all!

APOSTOLIC ALIGNMENT FOR PROPHETIC FULFILLMENT

God's perfect governmental structure causes reformation and produces transformation in the earth realm. His perfect order in His government cannot be resisted by the desolation of our lands. A land goes into desolation when its people transgress, sin, fall into idolatry, and deviate from God's ultimate plan. Once this deviation occurs, demonic forces have the right to establish themselves in the land and hold territories captive. In Scripture, there are four main categories of defilement of the land: *covenant breaking, idolatry, immorality, and unjust bloodshed*. When Joel wrote about the locusts entering the land of Judah and devouring both the land and people, all these defilements had occurred (see Joel 1:3-7).

In *God's Now Time For Your Life*, Rebecca Wagner Sytsema and I share:

> Our gift must work within the order that God has prescribed. Therefore, prophets, who are second in the order, must align their prophetic revelation with apostles, who are first in the order. This will produce prophetic fulfillment. The word "first" means "prototype" or "model." Therefore, what God is saying, prophesying or promising to us individually, corporately, territorially and generationally can only be modeled properly in this alignment. When our promises are aligned properly in God's divine

governmental order, we will see the harvest of the promises in the field where we are planted.[6]

A NEW REFORMATION ON THE HORIZON

The time has come again for a great new move of God to sweep the earth. One of my predominant calls in the Body of Christ is to realignment. This creates a new order in preparation for this move to begin. When we move toward reforming a society, we enter a new war season. To be successful in this season, we need a new alignment and method of gathering together and "doing church."

I was involved in the cell movement when I was on the staff of a Baptist church in the 1970s and 1980s and saw many of the pitfalls and benefits of cell ministry. After moving my family to Denton, Texas (where our ministry is located today), we connected with Robert Heidler. As he and I began moving forward together in ministry, we incorporated cell groups into our vision, knowing that small groups were key. However, because of extensive travel and other demands, I lost sight of the call in the new millennium and our *"cell groups"* just rocked along.

I watched as many who had found their prophetic gifting were squelched in the traditional church; they needed to be reconnected. Others in many areas around the United States and even internationally did not have viable churches at all. As a result, they were scattered or isolated.

The Spirit of God spoke to me and said, *"Tell My people to **be sure you are aligned somewhere!** Develop a plan to gather the scattered sheep."* At that point, the call of our ministry, Glory of Zion International, changed. We became a prophetic, apostolic ministry that ministers throughout the world. Over the last three decades I had been used to help establish a worldwide prayer army. Now, the Lord seemed to be saying to me, *"Help Me gather My people in a new way!"*

When God speaks, things change and take on a different identity! All of us called to minister to God's people must be creative as we develop His wineskin for the future. One thing the Lord asked me to initiate in our ministry is what we call *Zion Connect*, which uses technology to allow individuals to connect *functionally*. I found that the Internet and Web-based communication were wonderful tools for worldwide connection and communication. If I could find these scattered and isolated people, they could use their computers to connect in a new, functional way in their homes. By gathering in their homes and watching our webcasts to better hear "what the Spirit is saying to the Church," "the scattered sheep" could have an avenue to hear the word and then pray for their territories in a new way. *With the Web, I knew what I was to do. I am a connector and mobilizer. Once He said, "Gather," I was ready to do so.* As a result, we now attempt to care for 10,000 new sheep that have aligned here and to oversee almost 6,000 house churches.

USING THE TOOLS OF SOCIETY

Church is a gathering where we fellowship. However, church is more than people gathered for fellowship. Church is a gathering to gain war strategies so we triumph against the enemy that Jesus came to destroy (see 1 John 3:8). Church is the viable organism that God uses to advance His Kingdom. The original warring unit that God designed in the beginning was the family (see Gen. 1:28). I believe that is why the enemy attempts to destroy families and the concept of family by using mega-gatherings where no one seems touched. The functional connecting of giftings is just as important as the territorial or local fellowship. Even though I travel as much as three weeks out of the month, I want to stay connected with my local church family. I also want to attend the prophetic prayer gatherings, involving people worldwide, that go on during the week. I have a burning desire to stay connected, and our Internet webcasts have provided this opportunity.

Zion Connect was designed to keep the Body connected and communicating via the Internet so that all of us could better develop and mature in our gifts. Many with intercessory, prophetic giftings now have a way to connect and can once again reach out to others around them and in their communities. This is reformation. Therefore, our ministry, Glory of Zion, has become a gathering place for many who are called to a more reformational way of doing church. We have taken the barriers off the Church and not limited our gathering to four walls. We believe the Church invades every culture of life and can transform society in days ahead. We are asking the Lord for an alignment reformation to occur worldwide.

A TESTIMONY AND EXHORTATION

God's ultimate intent was for the Garden to be filled with His glory. His glory would then work its way out and cover the entire earth. This is still His purpose today, but we are working from a standpoint of restoration. Land needs glory to represent the fullness of God. So when a people develop a nation and align that nation with God's covenant plan, they start the restoration process of bringing God's glory into the earth realm. However, when they divert from God's covenant plan, the glory lifts and decay begins. Therefore, we have other elements that we must process before we will see restoration occur. We must deal with illegal bloodshed, idolatry, immorality, and covenant breaking. Any time these issues enter into God's covenant relationship and plan for a nation, they have to be addressed, and reconciliation has to occur.

Recently, I received this letter from John Price, an apostolic leader in New Jersey. He and his wife, Sheryl, are aligned with Peter Wagner and me. They mobilize their state in many ways for reformation. They have testimony after testimony describing how the Lord has moved in the state of New Jersey. New Jersey is the Garden State and is one of the best examples of restoring and reforming the "Garden" in America. He writes:

> In Numbers 11 we see Israel complaining to Moses about not having meat. God's response to Moses was two-fold: "Gather 70 elders to share the burden of this people", and "You'll eat meat till it comes out of your nose". God seemed to be saying to Moses, "I am weary with this people and now I will not be requiring you to deal with them by yourself any longer." Numbers 11:16 and 17 gives us a clear understanding of how God was aligning and structuring His people. When you translate this passage it reads, "Assemble and put together your brothers (and sisters) so I can heap the anointing I have put on you, onto them, and marry them to my plan."
>
> In verse 24 of this same chapter, we see Moses "placing" the elders around the tabernacle. The word "placed" means "to stand in relationship with." When they were standing in proper relationship, watch what happens to them—the LORD comes down in a cloud and places the same anointing on the 70 that was on Moses. When the Spirit rested on these placed ones, they prophesied. In Numbers 11:25, the word "gave, or placed" here means to frame, hang up, ordain, or pour. The word "rested upon" means "cause to be"!
>
> Up until this point, they had been watching Moses move and operate in a realm of the Spirit that they themselves had never moved in or experienced. They

were like many of us. We watch a minister and stand in awe of their anointing, never once considering that God wants us to experience the same revelatory flow. The reason you frame a picture and hang it up is for others to see it. A picture is worth a thousand words. Instead of just looking at the picture, the Lord wanted them and us today to become part of the picture.

Interestingly, two of the elders were separated from Moses and the other 68 elders. Why they were not there is not written. However, notice something, when the release of the Spirit of prophesy that fell on Moses and the 68 elders in the Tabernacle occurred, something happened to the two not there. The Spirit of God also fell on the two elders in the camp! THEY PROPHESIED, too! (verse 26) Their names were Eldad and Medad, and the Word of God states they were among those listed. Eldad means "God has loved," and Medad means, "loving affection." Even though the camp (reserve or army) was murmuring and complaining about how God was providing for them, He still demonstrated His love and affection for them by causing Eldad and Medad to prophesy in the camp. This was the medicine prescribed by the Great Physician to try to help them get out of the mess they had gotten themselves into.

Now, look what the reaction was to God moving among His people in a new expression of His love and affection. In Verses 27 and 28, a young man goes to Joshua and "rats on" Eldad and Medad. Joshua, in turn, ran to Moses, in a tizzy, requesting that Moses FORBID THEM. The use of "young man" in this account means "baby," and "choice man," referring to Joshua, means "youth." Much could be said here, but the major point is that when a new move of God breaks out in unusual ways, babies and the spiritually immature start screaming about it—especially when it's not being released in a familiar fashion.

Moses had the right response! He stated that he wanted everyone to experience the outpouring of God's Spirit. Verse 29 says, "Would to God that all the Lord's people were prophets and He would put His Spirit upon them." "Would" and "would put" are the same Hebrew word meaning "to flow, to frame, to hang up." God was trying to get Israel to see the big picture—not just what was on the menu for the day. Moses response was in line with Paul's teachings in 1 Cor. 14:31,39, "For you can all prophesy in turn so that everyone may be instructed and encouraged.... Therefore, my brothers, be eager to prophesy, and do not forbid speaking in tongues." So we see that when the 70 elders stepped into the picture by standing in relationship with Moses and one another (aligning), the Spirit of Prophesy fell. It didn't matter that they weren't physically in the same place. God released a message from the Throne expressing His love and affection to help them understand His desire to stand in covenant relationship with them (marry) and to establish His Kingdom plan. There has never been a more critical time to examine with whom you are aligned. Whatever anointing they are flowing in will be heaped on you and YOU WILL PROPHESY!! Whatever wine they are drinking will be poured out on you! And not just once (like the elders) since we now have a better covenant! Sheryl and I are very grateful to be aligned with Dr. Chuck Pierce and Dr. Peter Wagner. Heap it on me LORD!![7]

A PROPHECY

At Glory of Zion, we meet at least three times a week and pray. We have people in over 120 nations that meet with us on the Web. One of the key components of our prayer meetings is prophetic utterance. In a prayer meeting, this word came forth:

> **This is a time to know My presence.** *This is a time to know My ark and to know what ark you are to enter to journey into your future. I am causing My presence to flood in the land. Raise your sail and watch the glory begin to take you to a new place. Don't hesitate. Hesitation is set as a snare to My movement for your life. Let your faith push you and catapult you. When you hear the wind of truth being spoken into a situation, move immediately. You don't want to miss the boat. You don't want to miss your proper alignment. Don't hesitate. Delay is set as a trap. The word is critical in this hour. The intensity that is behind the word is pushing you forward at speeds and levels that we know not of, so don't hesitate and don't fall for the trap.*
>
> **Within the sands of your desert, there is a highway.** *But in the sands of your desert you have grown accustomed to the atmosphere and the sirocco wind that has been around you. In the sands of your desert, create a new atmosphere, and I will cause that highway that is*

down deep to rise up. For there are ways of escape for My people in this next season. There are ways of escape that are forming, but you must create the wind that causes the highway to rise in front of you. I am laying the road. I am laying a road. Watch it form now. Go with Me on this new road, for you are headed into a place that you have not been. You must bring forth the wind and create the road so that you can end up where I have called you to be—new businesses, new alignments, new assignments.

I'm having you to return *to some business associates that you separated from and chose to walk a different direction from in this past season. Even now you will go back and reform a new way to venture forward. New ventures are on the horizon for My people. You must now grab hold and get on a highway that sets you ahead of the curve. You will go back and re-form a plan with them like Paul went back and got John Mark. These relationships will no longer be the same, but will be brought under a new covenant plan. They were once in an old structure, but now will be brought into a new structure. If those relationships are unwilling to come into a new structure, move on down the road for there are new relationships that will create this new venture. I will give some opportunities that did not manifest in the past season and now they will have an opportunity for a manifestation in this season. The ventures of My people now will take a shift in their formation. Realign and then align again so that those ventures might manifest properly!*

A TOUR TO ALIGN A NATION FOR REFORMATION

Dutch Sheets and I have been friends for years. We would always find ourselves ministering at conferences, speaking in various places, or being in prayer meetings together. We were at a conference in Washington, D.C., in October 2002, and separately the Lord called us to align our gifts, apostle-prophet, and travel to all 50 states in America. We called this the Fifty-State Tour.

We held meetings in each state, and people would come from all over the state, and we would minister. We communicated what God was doing in the Body of Christ in our nation, and then prophesied to each state. In each state, Dutch would discuss time and realignment. His main message to the nation was: *"God is snapping many things back in order that have been out of order."* Then he would proceed to teach about time. His favorite Scripture was Isaiah 46:10, which says, *"Declaring the end from the beginning, and from ancient times things that are not yet done, saying, 'My counsel shall stand, and I will do all My pleasure.'"* Another version of this verse says, *"My purpose will be established, and I will accomplish all My good pleasure"* (NASB). He always tied this verse to Job 22:28: *"You will also decree a thing, and it will be established for you; and light will shine on your ways"* (NASB). In other words, he was teaching that you can decree a thing, and it will manifest and give light to your path. God can show you something He declared in the past; when you pronounce that declaration into another time frame, then in that season, light comes and explodes in your path.

Together, we wrote a prophetic history book called *Releasing the Prophetic Destiny of a Nation.* In that book, I share:

> A decree is an official order, edict, or decision. A de-
> cree is something that seems to be foreordained. This
> is what makes decrees prophetic. Decree can also

mean to order, decide, or officially appoint a group or person to accomplish something. A decree is linked with setting apart or ordaining something or someone. A declaration is the act of announcing something or making a formal statement or proclamation. This statement sometimes is what a plaintiff releases in his complaint resulting in a court action. A *proclamation* actually brings something into a more official realm. A proclamation can ban, outlaw, or restrict. This is linked with the process of binding and loosing.

Once we hear the word of the Lord decreed, declared, or proclaimed, God begins to establish this word in the earth realm. This causes God's people to press in for a full manifestation of what He is longing to accomplish in our midst. All through the Word of God you find decrees, declarations, and proclamations. Cyrus sent out a decree that caused God's people to return from captivity and rebuild the city of Jerusalem and the temple of God. Caesar sent out a decree that positioned Mary and Joseph in the place where prophecy could be fulfilled through the birth of Jesus. Elijah declared that the heavens would be shut up. The priests proclaimed what God was ordaining.[8]

For this or any nation to be transformed and for reformation to occur, God's order must first be established in each state. When strategic intercessors are aligned with apostolic leaders, breakthrough begins. Intercessors carry the burden of God, prophetic people make key declarations, and apostles set the decrees in motion. In other words, intercessors keep the heavens open; prophets begin to express God's heart, making key declarations into the atmosphere; and apostolic leaders pull upon that revelation or blueprint of Heaven and bring it into an established form in the earth realm.

Each time you come into agreement with Heaven and speak the will of the Father into the earth, God's eternal time and plan resequences and realigns the earth. I believe that this is the most important concept of alignment that we need to understand. We are living in a time when the will of Heaven is being communicated to God's prophets and apostles of this age. This is releasing an overpowering strength in His people that is causing the headship of the god of this world to be subdued.

HEAVEN AND EARTH ARE REALIGNING

As we explained at the beginning of this chapter, there is a *katartizo*—a shift or adjustment of the earth back into its God-appointed purpose and destiny. This shift is beginning in the House of God, but affecting the whole earth. This spiritual shift is causing nations to realign. God's people, who are part of His headship to rule the earth, are now developing a new authority that reflects His rule and dominion. Due to the positive effects of much prayer, fasting, repentance, and so forth on the part of many, it is now time for the fruit of these actions to occur: realignment, repairing, rebuilding, restoring, and healing.

Intercessors are standing in the gap for nations to be healed rather than destroyed, and broken places are being katartisis-ed—realigned spiritually—with the plan and purposes of God (see Ezek. 22:30-31). This is reformation. This creates transformation. History is being healed; destiny is being reconnected. We must continue to prophesy, pray, and decree. This causes us to better understand the curse, as well as launch nations into new levels of blessing. God is realigning and positioning nations to see a worldwide move of God. This will result in many salvations and the turning of nations back to God and their destiny. Curses are being broken, blessings are being released, and our God-given voice is being restored.

This is a reformational shift. A shift is a change of place, position, or direction. A shift also includes an exchange, or replacement, of one thing for another. A shift is a change of gear so that we can accelerate. A shift can also be an underhanded or deceitful scheme. Therefore, in our shift, we must recognize that the enemy is plotting to stop it. God is ready for us to shift through our choice to enter into a new dimension of faith. Let us not lean on our understanding, but shift into this new dimension of faith.

In *Interpreting the Times*, I share the significance of understanding the times we are living in:

> The greatest change in this hour of history is in heavenly places. We are living in interesting times. These days seem like dangerous times, but actually they are times when the Lord is developing His men and women of faith who will rule and take dominion. Heaven and Earth are in a divine realignment. Revelation 12:7-9 says:

> *Then war broke out in heaven; Michael and his angels went forth to battle with the dragon, and the dragon and his angels fought. But they were defeated, and there was no room found for them in heaven any longer. And the huge dragon was cast down and out—that age-old serpent, who is called the Devil and Satan, he who is the seducer bv   deceiver) of all humanity the world over; he was forced out and down to the earth, and his angels were flung out along with him* (Revelation 12:7-9 AMP).

The obedience of the Lord Jesus Christ to be a sacrifice for mankind secured the triumph over the
dragon. However, today we are still engaged in the
conflict to enforce the right of dominion that we have
been given. The more you pray and cry out to the
Lord, the more He pushes the enemy into your sphere
of authority in the earth realm. So when the enemy
manifests against you or shows up in your path, this
is because you are on the verge of winning a great war
against him, or because you are at a place of birth-
ing your next vision. This is the time that you should
shout, "NOW salvation and strength have come!" The
manifestation of your resisting the tactics of the enemy is one of the key road signs that you are walking
in victory and entering a NOW season. You have entered into a new time frame, and as Revelation 12:12
says, "He knows that his time is short" (NIV).[9]

How do we do this? How do we rebuke this level of demonic
forces? This is where we get back to boundaries and to our proper
covenant place. When God gives the Church in a city the right order
of government and gifting, when the Church begins to come into
proper order, we then have the authority to dethrone the thrones
of iniquity that rule in our cities. Many times in Scripture, people
mixed the worship of God and idols. God does not tolerate divided
loyalties. Therefore, He said to Israel, *"...I will destroy your high
places. Then your altars shall be desolate..."* (Ezek. 6:3-4; see also Num.
33:52). The Lord showed the Israelites that they would need to drive
out from within their boundaries any form of worship that did not
lead them to Him. If they did not, this divided form of worship
would deplete their faith and cause them to lose their spiritual and
physical blessings.

In times of restoration under the Old Covenant, God commanded those in governmental authority to tear down high places. Those who did so prospered; those who did not were judged. Under the New Covenant, the Lord has given us access through His Spirit to dismantle the things in the heavens that are holding back His inheritance for a territory. We are to war with the powers and principalities that are withholding blessings. The Lord will clothe us in authority and release to us power that will cause His glory to be seen all over the earth.

JOSIAH

God is always raising up people on earth to overthrow satanic systems of worship. He has given us examples of such people and their strategies throughout the Bible. Consider King Josiah: *"Now before him there was no king like him, who turned to the Lord with all his heart, with all his soul, and with all his might, according to all the Law of Moses; nor after him did any arise like him"* (2 Kings 23:25). Josiah dethroned the thrones of iniquity of his day. He overthrew the satanic system of worship, in order that God might once again be worshiped in the land. He was a reformer. He restored order. He realigned the nation with the Word of the Lord and His covenant plan for Israel. When you read Second Kings 22–23, you will see eight things that Josiah did to restore God's order. In *The Future War of the Church*, Rebecca Wagner Sytsema and I share from the life of Josiah on how we can align ourselves with God's purposes and each other to see reformation:

> 1. **Josiah acknowledged the problem.** When Josiah began to have repairs made to the Temple, the high priest Hilkiah revealed that he had found a book of Law that was brought and read

to Josiah. In hearing the Law read, Josiah realized his forefathers had not followed God's law.

2. **Josiah humbled himself and repented.** Even though the Bible does not record that he had personally been involved in disobedience to the Lord, Josiah humbled himself and repented before the Lord for the actions of his forefathers. Today we would call this identificational repentance.

3. **Josiah inquired of the Lord.** He then had the high priest inquire of the Lord on his behalf and on behalf of the people of Judah concerning the Law. Inquiring of the Lord was a strategy of war that David used in his day, and it still has great power for those today who have an ear to hear what the Spirit is saying to us (see Rev. 2:29).

4. **Josiah received the word of God's prophet.** The prophetess Huldah then gave Josiah a word from the Lord. Her prophetic utterance told of how the Lord had been provoked to anger because the people had forsaken Him and burned incense to other gods. During the past several years, the Lord has been restoring the gift of prophecy to the Body of Christ. Paul tells us to desire the gift of prophecy (see 1 Cor. 14:1). Amos 3:7 says, *"Surely the Lord God does nothing, unless He reveals His secret to His servants the prophets."* Josiah understood, as we

must today, that prophecy will help us to understand a problem and point us in the direction the Lord is requiring of us.

5. **Josiah made declarations about the law of God.** Lawlessness causes spiritual chaos. When Josiah came to the throne, spiritual chaos and idolatry had taken over the land. After hearing from the book of the Law and hearing the voice of the prophet, Josiah then gathered all the people, both great and small, and had the Law read aloud. Not only was Josiah reviving the Law for the people; he was declaring God's covenant to the heavens.

6. **Josiah made a territorial commitment before God.** *"Then the king stood by a pillar and made a covenant before the Lord, to follow the Lord, and to keep His commandments and His testimonies and His statutes, with all his heart and all his soul, to perform the words of this covenant that were written in this book. And all the people took a stand for the covenant"* (2 Kings 23:3). Josiah knew his boundaries. He knew where his kingly authority extended and where it ended. And within those boundaries, he promised before God to perform the words of His covenant. All the people within that territory took a stand with Josiah.

7. **Josiah tore down the high places.** Josiah then did many physical acts within his sphere

of influence to see the throne of iniquity over-turned. He burned the articles made for the idol worship of Baal and Asherah (see 2 Kings 23:4). He removed the idolatrous priests who had been burning incense to Baal and the sun, moon and stars (see 2 Kings 23:5). He burned the idol of Asherah that had been placed in the Temple (see 2 Kings 23:6). He tore down the houses where the Temple prostitutes had been located (see 2 Kings 23:7). He destroyed the pagan al-tars placed on the rooftops (see 2 Kings 23:12). He confronted high-ranking demonic spirits such as Ashtoreth, Chemosh, and Milcom (see 2 Kings 23:13). He wiped out idolatrous high places and executed the priests who would not repent (see 2 Kings 23:19-20). He also punished anyone who had consulted with mediums or spiritists (see 2 Kings 23:24).

8. **Josiah restored true worship.** Josiah then com-manded that all the people keep the Passover, which had not been held since the days of the judges (see 2 Kings 23:22). Once the throne of iniquity is overturned, the throne of God needs to be established over an area in order to see it transformed and God's covenant established in the land.[10]

UNDERSTANDING THIS TIME OF REALIGNMENT

We are in a time of realignment. God is realigning the genera-tions (see Isa. 59). He is realigning your borders and boundaries! He is realigning your sphere of authority. He is snapping into place and securing your covering. He is opening up and realigning your vision. He is beginning to align your future, so that your past will be overtaken and healed. He is adjusting and realigning the blueprint for the building plan of your future. He is mending your storehouses and showing you how to prepare more! He is realigning the sounds of Heaven with the sounds of earth. He is realigning each one of us with His authority structures and then aligning all of us together as His Body in a new way. This is reformation. Once this is complete in this season, we will see His Spirit flow from this unity and break every yoke of bondage in each area of societal culture. Let the holy Chiropractor do His work!

Endnotes

CHAPTER 1: THE LOVE REFORMATION—JOHN ARNOTT

1. Quoted in Brennan Manning, *The Furious Longing of God* (Colorado Springs, CO: David C. Cook, 2009).

CHAPTER 2: UNASHAMEDLY HOLY—CINDY JACOBS

1. Sergio Scataglini, *The Fire of His Holiness* (Ventura, CA: Renew, 1999), 37.

2. Jerry Bridges, *The Pursuit of Holiness* (Colorado Springs, CO: NavPress, 1978), 19.

3. A.W. Pink, *The Doctrines of Sanctification* (Swengen, PA: Bible Truth Depot, 1955), 25.

4. C. Peter Wagner, *Radical Holiness for Radical Living* (Colorado Springs, CO: Wagner Press, 1998, 2002), 12.

5. Joy Dawson, *Intimate Friendship with God: Through Understanding the Fear of the Lord* (Grand Rapids, MI: Chosen Books, 1986, 2008), 18-19.

6. *Ibid.*, the four levels are excerpted from pages 67-71.

7. Cindy Jacobs, *The Reformation Manifesto: Your Part in God's Plan to Change Nations Today* (Grand Rapids, MI: Bethany House Publishers, 2008).

8. Graham Power, "Unashamedly Ethical Individual Commitment Form," *Unashamedly Ethical,* http://unashamedlyethical.com/CommitmentForm/?form=Individual (accessed March 8, 2010).

9. "A City on a Hill," *Fellowship Chapel,* http://fchapel.com/city.htm (accessed March 8, 2010).

CHAPTER 3: HISTORY BELONGS TO THE INTERCESSORS—JAMES W. GOLL

1. James W. Goll, *The Prophetic Intercessor* (Grand Rapids, MI: Chosen Books, 2006), 24.

2. *Merriam-Webster's Collegiate Dictionary*, 10th Edition, s.v. "Intercession."

3. James Strong, *Strong's Exhaustive Concordance of the Bible* (Peabody, MA: Hendrickson Publishers, n.d.), s.v. "Lead" (Hebrew #5608).

4. James W. Goll, *Praying for Israel's Destiny* (Grand Rapids, MI: Chosen Books, 2005).

CHAPTER 4: GOING FROM GLORY TO GLORY—BILL JOHNSON

1. Daniel Goleman, Richard Boyatzis, and Annie McKee, *Primal Leadership: Realizing the Power of Emotional Intelligence* (Boston: Harvard Business School Press, 2001), 7-9.

CHAPTER 5: CREATING A CULTURE OF LIFE—LOU ENGLE

1. Patrick Cormack, *Wilberforce: The Nation's Conscience* (Basingstoke, Hants, England: Pickering & Inglis Ltd, 1983), 54.

2. Judge John Noonan, "Single Issue Voting," *Georgia Right to Life* December 7, 2009, http://www.grtl.org/politicalaction.asp (accessed March 11, 2010).

3. "Abortion Statistics," *National Right to Life Educational Trust Fund* (Jan 2008), http://www.nrlc.org/Factsheets/FS03_AbortionInTheUS .pdf (accessed March 11, 2010).

4. Sam Brownback, *Iowa Straw Poll Speech* (Ames, IA: Hilton Coliseum, Aug. 11, 2007), video, http://www.election.tv/Samuel_ Brownback/videos/582/Iowa_Straw_Poll_Speech_by_Sam_ Brownback (accessed March 11, 2010).

5. Rob Bell, *Velvet Elvis* (Grand Rapids, MI: Zondervan, 2005), 68.

6. Martin Luther, quoted in "Diet of Worms," *Encyclopædia Britannica Online,* http://www.britannica.com/EBchecked/topic/649151/Diet-of -Worms (accessed March 11, 2010). Emphasis is author's own.

7. Diane S. Dew, "Margaret Sanger: In Her Own Words," quoting from *Women and the New Race* (Eugenics Publ. Co., 1920, 1923), http://www.dianedew.com/sanger.htm (accessed March 11, 2010).

8. Rob Stein, "U.S. Birthrate drops 2 percent in 2008," *Washington Post* (April 7, 2010) http://www.washingtonpost.com/wp-dyn/content/article/2010/04/06/AR2010040600758.html (accessed April 16, 2010).

9. "In the News," *Bound4LIFE,* http://bound4life.com/in-the-news (accessed March 11, 2010).

10. Imam Abdul Alim Musa, *The Third Jihad,* Dr. Zuhdi Jasser, Zuhdi, Film Director (Public Scope Films, 2008).

11. Hope's Treasure Orphan Care Family Counsel (Montgomery, AL: 2008).

12. Check out www.thezoefoundation.com for more details.

13. Every Child Deserves a Family Act (H.R. 3827) http://www.rothman.house.gov/index.php?option=com_content&task=view&id=1175&Itemid=1 (accessed August 30, 2010).

14. Ashcroft and Thomas, *On My Honor* (Nashville, TN: Thomas Nelson Publishers, 2001), 188.

15. Elliot A. Edward, "Out of the Blue," *Guideposts* (2008), http://www.guideposts.com/story/mysterious-ways-bakht-singh-christian-leader (accessed March 11, 2010).

16. Patrick Cormack, 68.

17. Leon Wood, *A Commentary on Daniel* (Eugene, OR: Wipf & Stock Publishers, 1998), 131.

18. Arthur Mattews, *Born For Battle* (Wheaton, IL: Harold Shaw Publishers, 1978), 22.

19. Lydia Saad, "More Americans 'Pro-Life' than 'Pro-Choice' for First Time," *Gallup Poll* (May 15, 2009), http://www.gallup.com/poll/118399/More-Americans-Pro-Life-Than-Pro-Choice-First-Time.aspx (accessed March 11, 2010); "Public Takes Conservative Turn on Gun Control, Abortion," *The Pew Research Center for the People and the Press* (April 30, 2009), http://people-press.org/report/513/ (accessed March 11, 2010); and "Support for Abortion Slips," *The Pew Forum on Religion and Public Life* (Oct. 1, 2009), http://pewforum.org/docs/?DocID=441 (accessed March 11, 2010).

20. Steven Ertelt, "Pro-Life Group Will Help 650 Pregnancy Centers Get Ultrasound Machines," *Lifenews.com* (April 22, 2005), http://www.lifenews.com/nat1293.html (accessed March 11, 2010).

21. *Ibid.*

22. Peter Marshall and David Manuel, *Sounding Forth the Trumpet* (Grand Rapids, MI: Fleming H. Revell, 1997), 58.

23. *Ibid.*, 363.

24. Kenneth Davis, *Don't Know Much About History: Everything You Need to Know About American History* (New York: HarperCollins, 2003), 203.

25. Theodor Seuss Geisel, *Horton Hears a Who* (New York: Dr. Seuss Enterprises, Random House, 1954, renewed 1982), 6.

26. Rebecca Porter,, "Abortion Didn't Solve Anything," *Dakota Voice* (August 18, 2008), http://www.dakotavoice.com/2008/08/abortion -didnt-solve-anything/ (accessed April 16, 2010).

27. Matthew Lockett, Director of Bound4LIFE, http://www.bound4life .com.

CHAPTER 6: REFORMATION OF MARRIAGE—JIM GARLOW

1. Gavin Newsom, quoted in Karen Ocamb, "EQCA Raises Over $1.6 Million in 15 Minutes to Fight Antigay Ballot Initiative," *The Bilerico Project* (Aug. 5, 2008), http://www.bilerico.com/2008/08/ eqca_raises_over_16_million_in_15_minute.php (accessed March 11, 2010).

2. http://en.wikipedia.org/wiki/ Arizona_Proposition_102_ %282008%29 (accessed April 16, 2010).

3. http://en.wikipedia.org/wiki/ California_Proposition_8_ %282008%29#Results (accessed April 16, 2010).

4. CNN Politics, "Maine rejects same-sex marriage law," http://www .cnn.com/2009/POLITICS/11/04/maine.same.sex/ (accessed April 16, 2010).

CHAPTER 8: THE SEVEN MOUNTAIN MANDATE—LANCE WALLNAU

1. Loren Cunningham, *Making Jesus Lord: The Dynamic Power of Laying Down Your Rights* (Seattle: YWAM Publishing, 1989) 134-135.

2. Henry Kissinger, *Diplomacy* (New York: Simon & Schuster, 1999), 17.

CHAPTER 9: STEWARDING FOR REFORMATION—C. PETER WAGNER

1. Bruce Cook, "The Psychology of Investing," *Fund Raising Management* 29, no. 1 (March 1998).

2. Frank Damazio, *The Attitude of Faith* (New Kensington PA: Whitaker House, 2009), 133.

3. *Ibid.*, 154.

4. John Wesley, "Serving God with Mammon." http://www .cambridgestudycenter.com/giving/wesley.htm.l.

CHAPTER 10: ALIGNING FOR REFORMATION—CHUCK PIERCE

1. Dutch Sheets, *Intercessory Prayer: How God Can Use Your Prayers to Move Heaven and Earth* (Ventura, CA: Regal Books, 2008).

2. Spiros Zodhiates, *Hebrew-Greek Key Word Study Bible, New American Standard Bible* (Chattanooga, TN: AMG Publishers, 1977), 1846.

3. Dutch Sheets and Chuck D. Pierce, *Releasing the Prophetic Destiny of a Nation* (Shippensburg, PA: Destiny Image, 2005), 66.

4. *Ibid.*, 66-67.

5. Chuck D. Pierce, *God's Unfolding Battle Plan* (Ventura, CA: Regal Books, 2007), 21-22.

6. Chuck D. Pierce and Rebecca Wagner Sytsema, *God's Now Time For Your Life* (Ventura, CA: Regal Books, 2005), 66.

7. John Price, personal correspondence with the author, March 24, 2009.

8. Sheets and Pierce, 91-92.

9. Chuck D. Pierce, *Interpreting the Times* (Lake Mary, FL: Charisma House, 2008), 27-28.

10. Chuck D. Pierce and Rebecca Wagner Sytsema, *The Future War of the Church* (Ventura, CA: Regal Books, 2007), 137-139.

All Proceeds from the sale of this book will be
donated to Joseph Storehouse

"Joseph Storehouse" is a foundation established
to advance the Kingdom of God and bring
revival and reformation to society.

About the Authors

BILL JOHNSON
www.bjm.org
www.ibethel.org (his church's Website)

Bill and his wife Beni are the Senior Pastors of Bethel Church in Redding, California. He is a fifth generation pastor with a rich heritage in the things of the Spirit. He ministers internationally, teaching Jesus' life and message of reformation, bringing Heaven on the earth.

LANCE WALLNAU
www.lancelearning.com

Lance Wallnau is a recognized leader in the field of personal and organizational transformation. He directs the Lance Learning Group, a company dedicated to helping believers impact secular spheres by fully actualizing their gifts, talents, and skills within the sphere of their professional life.

CHUCK PIERCE
www.gloryofzion.org

Dr. Charles D. "Chuck" Pierce has been used by God to intercede and mobilize prayer throughout the world and is known for his accurate prophetic gifting which helps direct nations, cities, churches and individuals in understanding the times and seasons we live in. He serves as President of Glory of Zion International Ministries in Denton, Texas, and President of Global Spheres, Inc.

HEIDI BAKER
www.irisministries.com

Heidi Baker and her husband Roland are the founding directors of Iris Ministries, which oversees fifteen bases and has planted thousands of churches. Her ministry has been graced by an outpouring of the Lord's healing and miraculous power. Her passion is calling people into a radical place of intimacy with the Lord Jesus and on to their destinies in Him.

C. PETER WAGNER
www.globalharvest.org
www.wagnerleadership.org
www.apostlesnet.net

Peter Wagner is the Founder of the Global Harvest Ministries, the Wagner Leadership Institute, and the International Coalition of Apostles. His apostolic ministry regularly convenes strategic groups of apostles, prophets, deliverance ministers, and educators for social transformation. He taught at the Fuller Theological Seminary School of Intercultural Studies for 30 years, and he is the author of over 30 published works.

JAMES W. GOLL
www.encountersnetwork.com

Dr. James W. Goll is the president of Encounters Network and international director of Prayer Storm, and coordinates Encounters Alliance, a coalition of leaders. He ministers worldwide teaching and imparting the power of intercession, prophetic ministry, and life in the Spirit. He has written numerous books including *Prayer Storm, Angelic Encounters, Prophetic Intercessor, The Seer,* and multiple Bible study guides.

JOHN ARNOTT
www.Johnandcarol.org

John and his wife Carol are the Founding Pastors of Catch the Fire Toronto (TACF). He serves as President of Catch the Fire Ministries (CTF) and Overseer of Partners in Harvest (PiH), a network of churches. As international speakers, John has become known for his ministry of revival in the context of the Father's saving and restoring love.

CINDY JACOBS
www.generals.org

Cindy Jacobs is a respected prophet who travels the world ministering, not only to crowds of people, but to heads of nations. Perhaps her greatest ministry is to world influencers who seek her prophetic advice. Cindy has authored six books, *Possessing the Gates of the Enemy*, *The Voice of God*, *Women of Destiny*, *Deliver Us from Evil*, *The Supernatural Life*, and *The Reformation Manifesto*.

LOU ENGLE
www.louengle.com
www.TheCall.com

Lou Engle is the visionary and co-founder of TheCall solemn assemblies, a movement of prayer gathering young adults to pray and fast for breakthrough and revival. Lou Engle's heart passion is to call young adults into a lifestyle of radical prayer, fasting, and holiness and to pray, contending for the ending of the injustice of abortion and for righteous leaders to be raised up in America.

JIM GARLOW
www.jimgarlow.com
www.garlowperspective.com

Dr. Jim Garlow serves as Senior Pastor of Skyline Wesleyan. He is an author, communicator, and historian. Jim is heard daily on over 400 radio outlets nationwide in his one minute historical commentary called, "The Garlow Perspective." Jim's writings include: *Cracking Da Vinci's Code* (co-authored with Peter Jones) which has sold 350,000 copies, *How God Saved Civilization* (re-released as *God And His People*), *A Christian's Response to Islam*, *The Covenant*, *Partners in Ministry*, *The 21 Irrefutable Laws of Leadership Tested by Time*, *God Still Heals*, *The Da Vinci Code Breaker*, and a pocket-sized *Outline of the History of Christianity*.

In the right hands This Book will Change Lives!

Most of the people that need this message will not be looking for this book. To change their life you need to put a copy of this book in their hands.

> *But others (seeds) fell into good ground, and brought forth fruit, some a hundred-fold, some sixty-fold, some thirty-fold* (Matt. 13:3-8).

Our ministry is constantly seeking methods to find the good ground, the people that need this anointed message to change their life. Will you help us reach these people?

> *Remember this—a farmer who plants only a few seeds will get a small crop. But the one who plants generously will get a generous crop* (2 Cor. 9:6).

EXTEND THIS MINISTRY BY SOWING
3-BOOKS, 5-BOOKS, 10-BOOKS, **OR MORE TODAY,**
AND BECOME A LIFE CHANGER!

Thank you,

Don Nori Sr., Publisher
Destiny Image
Since 1982